Arabic Calligraphy

To
H.R.H. Prince Bandar bin Sultan
A True Symbol of the Saudi Spirit.

A Special Note

The Smithsonian Institution in Washington, D.C. hosted a series of lectures about Saudi Arabia during the spring of 1993. This collection is based on the presentations given in that lecture series. However, this collection has been edited and published by the Saudi Arabian Cultural Mission to the United States. The Cultural Mission is the sole owner of copyrights and is fully responsible for the articles printed herein.

Saudi Arabia
Tradition and Transition

A Lecture Series

edited by

Abdulaziz I. Al-Sweel
Saudi Arabian Cultural Mission to the United States
Washington, D.C.

and

J. W. Wright, Jr.
Washington College
Chestertown, Maryland

Printed in the United States of America

10 9 8 7 6 5 4 3 2 1

ISBN 1-881592-43-X

HAYDEN-MCNEIL PUBLISHING, INC.
6264 Hix Road
Westland, MI 48185
313-729-5550

Acknowledgements

The editors would like to thank the many people who helped with the organization of this collection of articles. Our deepest gratitude goes to H.R.H. Prince Bandar, Saudi Arabia's Ambassador to the United States, for sponsoring the Smithsonian program. His support made it possible for us to publish and distribute this collection. We also extend our sincere thanks to Dr. Hamad Al-Salloom, the Cultural Attaché, who was both encouraging and supportive of our work on this project. The many people at the Saudi Arabian Cultural Mission who helped to organize the lecture series also deserve our thanks. Our particular gratitude goes to Richard Bianchi and Afaf Yarcout.

As for the collection itself, we want all the contributors, readers, and reviewers to know how much their work is appreciated. We thank the contributors for volunteering to rewrite their lectures for printing as articles. In addition, each article was juried by a team of readers. The comments of Gerry Fischer, Mary Schmidt, Jefford Vahlbusch, Beverly Wolff and Diane Wright on drafts of articles have been very helpful. Dawn Baker's work typing the manuscript is greatly appreciated. Finally, our editors at Hayden-McNeil Publishers, Inc. deserve our thanks for helping with the layout of this book.

Prologue

Almost two years after the Gulf War, the Kingdom of Saudi Arabia is still the focus of many inquiries by the American public. Although oil trade and foreign direct investment have lead people to consider an American-Arab dialogue, the Gulf War piqued American interest in Saudi Arabian-United States policy relations. This rising interest about Saudi Arabia has allowed for the development of "Saudi Studies" forums and programs throughout the United States.

As a result, scholars on Saudi Arabia have been responsible for a noticeable increase in published materials on the Kingdom since the Gulf War. Of note in this regard are several recently published books: Abir Mordechai, *Saudi Arabia: Society, Government, and the Gulf Crisis*, Routledge, 1993; Joseph Kostiner, *The Making of Saudi Arabia, 1916-1936: From Chieftancy to Monarchical State*, Oxford University Press, 1993; Leslie McLoughlen, *Ibn Saud: Founder of a Kingdom*, St. Martin's Press, 1992; Ali N. Alghafis, *Universities in Saudi Arabia: Their Role in Science, Technology, and Development*, University Press of America, 1992; John R. Presley and Rodney Wilson, *Banking in the Arab Gulf*, Macmillan, 1991; and Aaron D. Miller, *Search for Security: Saudi Arabian Oil and American Foreign Policy, 1939-1949*, University of North Carolina Press, 1991.

Many published works, however, are not easily accessed by the general public or lay commercial and political leaders. For the most part, Saudi Arabia, a nation of astonishing contrasts, remains relatively unknown to most Americans. To help alleviate this situation, the Royal Embassy of Saudi Arabia's Cultural Mission in Washington, D.C. and the Smithsonian Institute jointly developed a lecture series for the Smithsonian's Campus on the Mall program. These educational sessions featured political analysts with intimate knowledge of the country's foreign affairs, scholars of Arab Studies, journalists who have lived in the Kingdom, and members of Saudi Arabia's religious establishment. Each speaker explored topics critical to a nation where centuries-old traditions must coexist with permanent and rapid change.

Saudi Arabia: Tradition and Transition is a collection of seven essays, with the addition of an introductory chapter and an epilogue, that are based on the presentations given at the Smithsonian's lecture series. Necessarily, the articles that are included in this book vary greatly in scope and tone. Some are essays based on personal experiences, others are academic in nature, and one presents an Imam's redefinition of "Islamic fundamentalism" in a Saudi Arabian context. All the articles represent attempts to provide the American public with clear and balanced information about Saudi Arabia, its culture, its people, and its politics. The book is divided into two sections. The first set of essays discusses the events that are forcing many Saudi traditions into a transitory stage of development. The second set of articles focuses on the Kingdom's efforts to preserve, and, in some cases, to renew ancient Arab traditions.

The contributors, editors, and sponsors of this collection believe that this unique approach to expanding Americans' knowledge on Saudi Arabia will be beneficial to many people. We would like to emphasize that the articles presented are based on academic lectures given at the Smithsonian Institution's Campus on the Mall. The book will be available to the public through the Saudi Arabian Cultural Mission to the United States. We expect that the book will be used by out-reach coordinators and training managers, and also as a text for courses on the Arab Middle East. Above all, we hope the collection facilitates dialogue between Saudi and American readers in a variety of fields.

Table of Contents

List of Photographs

List of Tables

Saudi Arabia: Tradition and Transition
An Introduction

Abdulaziz Al-Sweel

Later in this book, J. W. Wright makes the claim that Saudi Arabia without oil would be a very different place. This is, of course, true because revenues from oil sales finance the economic and infrastructure developments that are referred to in his article. But it is also true that Saudi Arabia without its peoples' strong commitment to community mores and traditions would be unable to handle rapid development. Although ours is a country and a culture whose basic bonds are found in civility, hospitality, and social justice, ours is also a society that for thousands of years has been able to accept and facilitate positive community, economic, and lifestyle change.

Since the 1970s, Saudi Arabia has raced toward modernization at a pace so fast that it tested our ability to maintain and share traditional systems of values. As a result of the clash between old world and new world lifestyle preferences, Saudi agencies are forced to remember their cultural, religious and social heritage when writing policies. Moreover, development administrators must build into their plans the recognition that our traditions are in transition. By "traditions" we mean peoples' loyalty to Islamic and Arab ideals, but also their commitment to social adaptability and flexibility. By "transition" we refer to fundamental changes in Saudi Arabia's economic base, in the forms and compositions of its community groups, and in the social regulations that affect individuals' interactions and statuses.[1]

The dual goals of preserving popular Arab traditions while building modern facilities for the general public have been the basis of every Saudi rulers' domestic agenda. The Kingdom of Saudi Arabia was founded by King Abdulaziz al-Saud in 1932 when he unified the Arabian Peninsula's tribal network into one system of governance. In 1933, the new King commissioned the first successful oil survey, and by 1938 he had established international relations with the world's great powers. King Abdulaziz's vision for making Saudi Arabia a developed country that was also free of colonial interference still influences the Kingdom's relationships with foreign commercial enterprises, governments, and international agencies.

Leadership of the country was passed to Abdulaziz's son, Saud, when the King died in 1953. Many of the government's central agencies were conceived during King Saud's eleven year rule. He is credited for creating a social welfare system, and he is remembered for his generosity to Islamic causes. King Saud was succeeded on the throne by his brother Faisal bin Abdulaziz in 1964.

It was during King Faisal's rule that the seeds of development planning were planted and when the first major breakthroughs in the country's industrialization process took place. More ministries and agencies were organized under his direction than had been created since the Kingdom's unification. His leadership built the formidable administrative and planning structures that allowed King Khalid bin Abdulaziz to implement the second and third development plans, after he became King following Faisal's death in 1975. Infrastructure development continued to accelerate during King Khalid's years on the throne, and the Saudi peoples' per capita income, educational sophistication, and social welfare rose to new heights.

King Fahd bin Abdulaziz assumed leadership of the Saudi monarchy in 1982 when King Khalid passed away. In King Fahd's years of rule, agriculture, education, and human resource development have received priority attention in national planning efforts. King Fahd has also been most generous in his support of Islamic institutions inside Saudi Arabia and abroad.

Today, the Saudi government operates as a monarchy that is beyond the control of any colonialist power. King Fahd acts as Prime Minister overseeing the deputies, ministers, and agency directors of the departments of state. One of King Fahd's major goals is to increase the involvement of the peoples of Saudi Arabia in their government process. In order to do this, he has organized a new Consultative Council that allows representatives from all regions of the Kingdom to discuss matters of local, national, and international concern. He and other key members of the royal family also make themselves available to the public through regular open forums. King Fahd's use of consensus and inclusion in the government's policy making process is outlined in Adel A. Al-Jubeir's article on politics in Saudi Arabia. Crown Prince Abdullah bin Abdulaziz is the Deputy Premier of Saudi Arabia and Head of the National Guard. Prince Sultan bin Abdulaziz is the Second Deputy Premier and Minister of Defense and Aviation. The Council of Ministers is responsible for national planning and policy implementation. In addition, the Kingdom's municipal structure is divided into fourteen regions that are headed by local governors.

The monarchy's government structure provides services to over twelve million Saudi citizens and to about four million expatriate residents. The Kingdom stretches over 865,000 square kilometers or eighty percent of the Arabian peninsula. Riyadh is the country's capital and its largest city, with a population in excess of two million people. Jeddah, the main commercial center on the Kingdom's west coast, also has a population of about two million people. Other main cities include Mecca, Medina, Abha, Buraidah, Dammam, Dhahran, Hail, Jubail, Tabouk (Taif), Unayzah, and Yanbu. Saudi Arabia shares the eastern coast of the Red Sea with Jordan and Yemen, and it shares the western coast of the Arabian Gulf with Kuwait, Oman, Qatar, and the United Arab Emirates.[2]

In addition to the development of the country's economy and government structure, there are constant efforts to preserve distinctly Arab traditions. One of the Kingdom's richest records of its traditions is found in its antiquities. Archaeologists have found artifacts and relics that are among the oldest in the world. Dr. Abdullah H. Masry has written an article about the ancient lands of Arabia and about the government's efforts to recover and restore its antiquities. Another record of the Saudi-Arab heritage is found in the region's oratory and poetic traditions. Nabati poetry is indigenous to the Nadj and it is a true reflection of the socio-political climate of the times. Dr. Saad Al-Sowayan's article is on the Arabs' use of festival tales and oral poetry as a means of preserving its history. This article also gives the reader a look at one of Saudi Arabia's major efforts to introduce the Kingdom's youth to ancient Arab traditions, the Grand Folk Festival at Al-Jenadriyah. Both of these articles will give insights into the millennia of traditions that filter their way into present-day society in Saudi Arabia.

The Kingdom's judicial system is based on a mixture of Islamic law, taken from the *Sharia*, and a body of legislation created by royal decree. The former are used to promote social justice and welfare to the community as a whole, while the later are issued to regulate the country's commercial and industrial activities. Within the government, the ministers maintain a serious commitment to the preservations of Muslim credos in the management of their organizations. This is not to say, however, that Saudi Arabia's Islamic government operates in a manor that is consistent with other, more militant Islamic governments. Indeed, Islamic doctrines are used in Saudi Arabia to promote a balance between government and religion. In his article on "Islam," Jaafer Idris tries to show how religious fundamentalism can play a positive role in Saudi Arabia.

We also wanted to look at the role of women in society. No socio-religious tradition has been more villified by the West than the role of a woman in Islamic and Arab societies.[3] It may also be true that no other tradition has been more misunderstood by people living outside the Saudi social structure. Therefore, former *Arab News* and *Saudi Gazette* correspondent Anne Marie Weiss-Armush has written an essay for the collection on her experiences as a woman who is married to a Moslem and who lived and worked in Saudi Arabia for eleven years. Her article suggests how and why the inclusion of women into all levels of Saudi Arabia's socio-economic structure is an important priority in the Kingdom's plans for the future.

The discussion of women's changing roles in Saudi society brings us back to my original thesis that efforts toward modernization must aim to promote well-being in every segment of society. The presence of new houses, paved highway systems, and super shopping malls might seem in striking contrast to a bedouin state's traditional lifestyle. There is no doubt that our commercial structure has changed and that the Kingdom's people are increasingly choosing to live in urban areas. But Saudi Arabia's new and modern physical facilities do not belie our real commitments to family, freedom, hospitality, and justice. When people in my parents' generation were born, for example, they could only expect to live thirty-seven years. Now, people in their age group can retire comfortably, they receive excellent medical attention from dedicated health care professionals, they eat food produced by Saudi farmers, and they can elect to receive income from one of the world's most generous social security programs. They can also rest assured that the King and his allies will protect them from the threat of military incursions.

My colleagues at the Saudi Arabian Cultural Mission to the United States and I can only speculate about the directions Saudi Arabian traditions will take in the future. In the Epilogue Richard Bianchi asks a number of provocative questions for readers to consider about Saudi Arabia's role in the twenty-first century's global economy. We all wonder what the answers to these questions will be. However, it seems doubtful to us that the Kingdom's new industrial complexes will lead to the discontinuation of Arab social mores. It is more likely that modernization will enable the Saudi people to make even greater contributions to the Arab world. This is, at the very least, the goal of Saudi Arabia's deputies, ministers and planners.

Notes

1. Soraya Altorki and Donald P. Cole, *Arabian Oasis: The Transformation of Unayzah* (Austin: U of Texas P, 1989) 1

2. Population estimates as released in the Royal Embassy of Saudi Arabia Commercial Office's *A Business Guide to the Kingdom of Saudi Arabia* (Washington, D.C., 1992).

3. J. W. Wright, "Women: Islam's Female Martyrs," *Dying for Love: The Discourse of the Female Martyr*, ed. Evan Blythin (Albany, NY: State U of New York P, forthcoming, 1993).

Saudi Arabia
The Forces of Transition

The Saudi State Today

by
Adel A. Al-Jubeir

The Kingdom of Saudi Arabia is often described as an outdated feudal monarchy which will not survive the twentieth century. As a Saudi who has worked closely within the system, and studied it intensely, I disagree. Let me set out for you an indigenous view of the Kingdom which may help explain both the stability and the resilience of the Saudi political order.

Studies of the Kingdom of Saudi Arabia have focused predominantly on oil and the associated wealth which comes with it. They have also tended to focus on the consequences of rapid modernization superimposed on a traditional milieu and often concluded with predictions of imminent social upheaval and political conflict. This has been especially true after the ouster of the Shah and the emergence of the Ayatollah Khomeini in Iran. All too often, these studies have relied on conceptual models devised at academic institutions far removed from the Kingdom's cultural, political, and social environment. The Kingdom's traditions, religion, and community structure are often ignored in favor of descriptions such as "closed" or "underdeveloped society" which imply a certain primitiveness when compared with Western industrial states. The notion is that because Saudi Arabia is "different from us" it cannot be as stable as us.

The monarchy is viewed by outside observers from a Western perspective. A monarchy in a traditional society is compared to a European monarchy of the Middle Ages, and just as these monarchies evolved into secular, democratic systems, the assumption is often that the Kingdom would have to go through the European process, the expectation is that it would be replaced through violent upheaval. The examples used to support this assumption are the collapse of monarchical systems throughout the Middle East in the 1950's, 1960's, and 1970's. Such descriptions, however, fail to take into account the historic and cultural factors unique to the Kingdom of Saudi Arabia. To understand the political system in Saudi Arabia, one must closely examine the context from which it emerged and the environment in which it operates. The context represents the historic and cultural background of a society, while the environment represents the time and place in which it operates.

The Historic Context of Saudi Arabia

The history of the Arabian Peninsula provides the context for understanding the political culture and the ways in which Saudi leaders and institutions have emerged in the twentieth century. Contrary to some observers, the histo-

ry of the Kingdom of Saudi Arabia does not begin with the 1973 oil embargo
or with the unification of the Kingdom by King Abdulaziz Al-Saud in 1932.
Rather it traces its beginnings to the formation of the first Saudi State in 1744,
thirty-two years prior to the American revolution. This first Saudi State
encompasses a geographic area roughly the size of the country today. It was
established on the basis of religion and ruled according to the Islamic Sharia
and tribal custom, in an area regarded as inhospitable to any comprehensive
political entity by its very nature. This was the first time, except for a brief
period at the time of the Prophet Mohammed, that the Arabian Peninsula was
unified under the banner of one state. Essentially, this state has endured —
under one leadership — to this day. It is a state which has been able to bring
together the various elements which make up the body politic of the
Peninsula: the tribes, farming communities, merchants, urban populations,
and religious elements. It is a state which derived its legitimacy from its
upholding of Islam and the teachings of the Prophet; a state which ruled with
the consent of its people.

Twice in its history, the state was destroyed by superior forces from outside the Peninsula, and twice it re-established itself in its domains. The first
Saudi state was destroyed in 1818 at the hands of Mohammed Ali of Egypt
and the second in 1891 by the power of the Ottoman Empire. Had it not been
for the legitimacy accorded to the state and its ruling family and the help and
support of the inhabitants of the Peninsula, it would have been inconceivable
for the Al-Saud family to re-emerge twice from defeat and re-establish a state.

I mention this historic aspect because it is important to an understanding
of the ways and means of the Kingdom today. Because the origins of the Saudi
state were based on the teachings of Islam, its rulers upheld certain values and
norms which provided for the efficient functioning of a civil society and, by
extension, the establishment of stability, order, and security without which no
state can remain viable. Islam and tribal customs provided the original blueprint for the establishment of the state. This blueprint, which has been
adhered to for over two centuries, has proven its resilience and viability, as
well as, its applicability to the environment of the Peninsula.

Let's take a look at this blueprint, at the heart of which lies the "social contract" between the sovereign and the people. In Islam, the social contract is a
very simple one: The people delegate power and pledge obedience to a sovereign in exchange for a commitment by the sovereign to uphold the Sharia and
to maintain stability, order, and security. It is more in the Lockean tradition
than the Hobbesian tradition. The ruler governs because of the legitimacy
accorded to him by his people, not the power granted him by his guns. The
Sharia provides for the protection of human rights, private property, and the
right of access to the ruler. It also lays down laws and rules of conduct and

behavior essential to the functioning of a civil society. In short, many of the elements associated with the United States Constitution and Bill of Rights are provided for in the Sharia. The question is whether or not the teachings of the Sharia are applied. In Saudi Arabia they are.

The tribal ethos of Saudi Arabia further decentralizes the structure of government: in a tribal society, little or no hierarchy is present. Nomadic societies cannot afford to create either elaborate government structures or a lot of pomp and ceremony around their leaders. The ruler is regarded as a first among equals and is judged by his ability to act as a mediator rather than arbitor of issues within the tribe. In addition to his piety, the Saudi ruler's bravery, intelligence, humility, and ability to forge consensus among the various elements of society are viewed as essential qualities. To achieve this, a ruler must consult and maintain open lines of communications with the rest of his community. When the tribal ethos is combined with the application of an Islamic form of government, what emerges is a system in which checks and balances prevail and in which open access between those who govern and those who are governed exists.

Philosophers from the time of Socrates and Aristotle in ancient Greece, and before that in the empires of Babalonia and Phoenicia, have discussed the nature and function of the state. They continue to do so today. Whether one adopts an ancient or modern view of the nature of the state, there is broad agreement regarding the constitution of "good" versus "bad" government: good government performs functions leading to the well-being of its citizens without causing them harm, while bad government either does not perform or does so while harming aspects of the lives of its citizens. The philosophy of governing in the Kingdom relies on winning the hearts of the people, not intimidating them. It is a philosophy of inclusion, not exclusion. One must be careful not to prejudice their views with ethnocentricity: the fact that others may have different community or social objectives does not mean that their ways are necessarily wrong or bad.

In examining the effectiveness of a political system, we should withdraw for a moment into the abstract. Let's forget the institutional makeup of the system (whether it is a democracy, theocracy, monarchy, or other form of government) and look at how a proper government should function. Essentially government is an input-output unit for transforming the demands of its people into actions meant to enhance their well-being. It is a "black-box" in which inputs (demands) are transformed into outputs. If the outputs of the system reflect the demands placed on it, the "black box" (government) is functioning. If they don't, it isn't. How the inputs are transformed into outputs depends on the particular system. In the U.S. you have elections; in Saudi Arabia we have an open system in which any citizen has the right to appear before the sovereign to plead his or her case, offer suggestions, make complaints, or simply to say "hello." The King holds a regular "majlis" for this purpose, as do all the regional governors and senior members of the royal family. Senior government officials must also allow open access to citizens. Through this open access, the government remains in touch with its people, becomes aware of their concerns, and takes steps to accommodate them.

Over the past two hundred and fifty years, the Saudi government has developed from a fairly simple structure into an increasingly complex one. The requirements of modern times have led it to make adjustments which allow it to function more effectively to serve its people.

The Environment in Which the Saudi States Operates

The environment, as I mentioned earlier, represents the time and place in which a political system operates. Saudi Arabia, by virtue of its geographic isolation, has been fortunate in not having experienced colonial rule. As a consequence, the struggle for independence experienced by many states in the Third World, as well as the creation of colonially-sponsored elites who themselves became mirror-images of their colonial masters, has been absent in Saudi Arabia. The Saudi political culture is essentially preserved from the past and its national identity forged by indigenous elites. The political system is organically linked to its natural geography and history. It is an evolution of its culture and not a transplanted model. Its key ingredients are Islam and tribal tradition.

The formation of the third Saudi state, which was initiated by King Abdulaziz in 1902 and completed in 1932, represents the emergence of the Kingdom of Saudi Arabia into the modern era. King Abdulaziz had the wisdom and foresight to realize that his nation could not be kept together unless it adapted itself to the requirements of modern times. He instituted a modern government and implemented development plans designed to enhance the lot of his people. He established a government bureaucracy where none has existed previously and set out to link his nation by means of a communications network designed to bring it closer together. He knitted together its Najdi heartland with the Hijaz in the West, the Asir in the South, and the oil-bearing provinces along the eastern seaboard. He established a standing army, radio broadcasting system, educational facilities, ties with outside powers, and he allowed for the exploration for oil with the hope that its fruits could be harvested to enhance the welfare of his people. He maintained stability, security, and peace in a land which had suffered from near anarchy and tyranny during the time when its natural leaders were destroyed by outside powers. His aim was to live up to his side of the bargain in the social contract. His hope was that his actions would improve the living conditions of his people and reconfirm their trust in their leadership. What he promised were not utopian ideals, but practical solutions to everyday problems. What he accomplished was not to create unfulfilled expectations, but real gains derived from the application of existing resources, no matter how modest those resources were at the time.

The philosophy of King Abdulaziz was maintained by his successors, and the Saudi state today proudly stands as a tribute to his wisdom and foresight. By the mid-1970's, the Kingdom's income allowed it to embark on more ambitious development plans. Between 1974 and 1990, the Kingdom invested over $800 billion on development projects. World-class schools and universities, roads, hospitals, ports, airports, industrial cities, and communications networks were built. The objective was to increase the well-being of all groups within the society and to foster social stability under circumstances of rapid social change. Human resources were developed by education, training, and an increased standard of living. Within the span of a few short decades, the quality of life in Saudi Arabia has been radically transformed.

If I may be permitted, here is an autobiographical note to illustrate this. My father was born the year before the formation of the third Saudi state was completed. The life expectancy of an average Saudi at birth was 37 years. Of his twenty siblings, fourteen survived. Of his contemporaries, 90 percent were illiterate. When a person fell ill, practitioners would treat him using traditional methods, with the chances of recovery slim. When people suffered from draught and hunger, locust often times offered the only means for survival. I was born thirty-one years later. The average life expectancy in the Kingdom had risen to 54 years. Of my ten siblings, all survived. Of my contemporaries, 70 percent could read and write. When I fell ill in my childhood, there were modest hospitals in which I could be treated. The days in which the consumption of locust was viewed as a means for survival were over. Mine was by far a better life than my father's. When my youngest sister was born, seventeen years after me, life expectancy had risen to over 60 years, and of her contemporaries, virtually all were literate. She had access to some of the most modern medical and educational facilities in the world. Today, her generation can look forward to a life of stability and prosperity. My personal story is not unique; it reflects the experience of Saudi families in general.

On a macro-level, the goal was to maintain high economic rates of growth, maximize earnings from oil over the long-term, and diversify the economy. Millions of foreign nationals, to whom we are grateful, helped in this endeavor, whether as doctors and engineers, educators and managers, or manual laborers. A vast American community put down roots among us. It has been with us since the 1930's. For all the talk about the insularity of the Kingdom, ours has been an open land. In fact, one of the largest civilian communities of

Americans living outside the U.S. resides in Saudi Arabia. All of this was achieved while maintaining the religious and moral values of Islam.

History shows that economic development and modernization can be ruthless invaders of traditional societies. Through the introduction of the basic elements of a welfare state and industrialization, the Saudi state has been able to impose a policy of controlled change without disrupting the traditional values of the society. The theme which has guided the Kingdom's development plans over the years has been "modernization without Westernization." Computers, factories, modern educational facilities, and super-highways, which represent the tools of modernity, were welcomed, while some of the Western life-styles, which have the potential for damaging the country's traditional religious character, were shunned. We did not commit the mistakes that were made by others. The state did not take it upon itself to herd the society into some alien world or to sever it from its roots. We knew, as Edmund Burke would have put it in a different context, that societies without a past are societies without a future.

The Saudi State Today

The Saudi state today is a reflection of the times in which it exists. It is dynamic and evolving. Its objective is to adapt itself to the requirements of the modern age without losing touch with its historic and cultural values. Saudi decision-makers have proven to be pragmatic and their approach to policy formulation has been innovative and closely compatible with changing circumstances. The government infrastructure is designed to allow for the most efficient functioning of government, given the Kingdom's geographic distribution. The government is divided into a national and regional structure. The national structure is headed by the King, while the regional structures are headed by governors. At the national level, the government is divided into an executive/legislative branch and a judicial branch. The two branches are independent of each other. The executive/legislative branch is managed through the Council of Ministers (cabinet), below which are the various Ministries and government bureaus. The judicial branch is headed by the Supreme Judicial Council, below which are the various courts and Courts of Appeal.

At the regional level are the provincial governments. There are fourteen provinces in the Kingdom, each headed by a governor, below which are the regions within the provinces, each headed by a sub-governor. The next level down are the cities, which are administered by mayors and the precincts within each city. This structure is similar in form and function to American state governments which operate at the level of the state, the county, the city, and the precincts.

The King is both Head of State and Head of Government. He symbolizes the unity of the nation and represents the supreme political authority in the land. His power, however, is circumscribed by the requirement that he adhere to the precepts of the Sharia which operates independently of the King and to which he himself is subject. In fact, in Saudi Arabia, the sovereign can be sued in his own courts. The King rules by consent, and virtually no important decision is made by him without extensive consultation with the various elements of society.

Saudi Kings are selected from the children and grandchildren of King Abdulaziz on the basis of ability. There is a meritocracy within the Royal Family. King Fahd, for example, has been closely involved with high-level government decision-making over the past forty-five years. He was a member of the Saudi delegation to the founding meeting of the United Nations in 1945. In 1953, he became the Kingdom's first Minister of Education. In 1963 he served as Minister of Interior, and in 1968 he became Second Deputy Prime Minister. In 1975 he was selected to be Crown Prince under the late King Khalid. From 1975 until his ascension to the throne in 1982, then-Crown Prince Fahd, in addition to being Deputy Prime Minister, chaired the Kingdom's Supreme Petroleum Council and the Supreme Council for Higher Education. He also maintained his ties with the religious establishment, the tribal chiefs, academics, merchants, and the general public. By the time he became King, he had established a track-record of domestic and international experience and achievement unmatched in the Kingdom.

In March of 1992, the Kingdom of Saudi Arabia introduced its Basic Laws of Government which essentially codified the customs which have existed in the Kingdom since its formation. The legal structure for a formal, independent, Consultative Council was created at the national level, as were legal structures for similar councils at the provincial level, to streamline the input mechanism.

It is important at this point to elaborate on the input mechanism and to describe how the state responds to input by the people. Input can come into virtually any level of the system; citizens may plead their cases to the mayors of the cities, the sub-governors of the regions, the governors of the provinces, Ministers, members of the Royal Family, or the King himself. If an issue is of paramount importance it is channelled immediately to the highest authority for action. This process also works in reverse and allows the state to accurately measure the pulse of the nation.

On August 2nd, 1990, Iraq invaded Kuwait and threatened the security of the Kingdom. The King was faced with the decision of whether or not to seek the assistance of outside powers. Within days, he was able to gauge the feelings of the Saudi public and determine that the vast majority feared an Iraqi advance into the Kingdom with all the accompanying destruction and horror wreaked upon Kuwait. The King also was able to determine that accepting assistance from outside powers would be welcomed by the public. By the time U.S. Defense Secretary Cheney arrived in the Kingdom on August 5th to offer assistance, outside observers, the so-called experts, were wondering whether the King would accept the assistance offered. When he did, some observers questioned the impact his decision would have on the Kingdom. They continued to question this issue during the build-up which culminated in the presence of over 600,000 foreign troops on Saudi soil. What those observers and commentators did not know was that the King was able, by virtue of the open channels in the Saudi system, to accurately assess the views of the Saudi public and respond to them accordingly. Those same observers wondered about the impact on Saudi society as Desert Shield turned into Desert Storm, and once again, they proved to be wrong, and the King right, in assessing that impact. Our society withstood the pressure — this vast armed presence, the scrutiny of a large press corps. Our people knew the stakes, and the political order emerged intact. I mention this example because it highlights the ability of the Saudi system to gauge its public opinion and to take measures in response. The King took actions knowing full well their consequences and not actions which he later had to worry about selling to the public.

Several weeks into the initial build-up, the presence of soldiers, both Saudi and foreign, became increasingly obvious in major urban areas throughout the Kingdom. Soldiers on leave would go into the cities and marketplaces carrying their weapons. Questions were raised by some citizens about their presence in the marketplaces: Was the Coalition expecting fighting to take place in the cities, and if so, what should the people do? Some shopkeepers, while pleased with the presence of added customers, expressed apprehension about the weapons they were carrying into shopping areas. Within days, these concerns had reached the King, and arrangements were made with the Coalition partners to require military personnel to conceal their weapons when entering urban areas.

These two examples illustrate the ability of the state to decipher the concerns of its citizens and to take measures to alleviate them. In the first example — the resort to outside assistance — the state needed to gauge the views of its citizens accurately, while in the second instance — the concealment of weapons — the citizens needed to make their concerns known and acted upon. The input-output mechanism worked. One does not require a profound crisis, such as Iraq's invasion of Kuwait, to illustrate the ability of the Saudi political system to reflect the views of its citizens. Rather, one can point to a host of other examples, such as the introduction of the radio in the 1940's and women's education and television in the 1960's, to show the ability of the system to introduce major social changes without disrupting society.

In the 1940's, King Abdulaziz sought to introduce radio broadcasting to enhance the Kingdom's communications network. A number of prominent citizens opposed the idea on the grounds that it was disruptive to society and would cause the faithful to deviate from the path of righteousness. In short, it was perceived to be the work of the devil. King Abdulaziz, by virtue of his position, could have forced the issue on society. What he did instead was to assemble those same notables who opposed the introduction of radio broadcasting and, at the time of prayer, turn the radio on. When the call to prayer was heard through the radio, King Abdulaziz asked those assembled how the work of the devil could carry the word of God? He indicated to them that the radio would be used to educate the faithful about their religion and about the world. Once the principle of the radio being beneficial to society was established, the rest was programming.

This approach did not differ from that taken by King Faisal in the 1960's when Saudi society was wrestling with the issue of women's education and the introduction of television. Television encountered the same resistance as the introduction of the radio had twenty years prior, and it was handled in a similar manner. Women's education, however, was more complicated. When King Faisal tried to establish schools for girls, some violently opposed the measure. King Faisal asked the religious establishment for a ruling on this issue. When the religious establishment supported his initiative, he decreed that any father had the right to prevent his daughters from attending schools and that the state would protect this right. At the same time, the state could not allow some to prohibit others from sending their daughters to school. To further reassure reluctant parents, he placed women's education under the guidance of the religious establishment. Once again, a principle was established, and the issue became one of selecting curriculums. Today, 50% of all students through the post-graduate level are females, and their curriculum does not differ from that of males.

Saudi Foreign Policy

What the above examples illustrate is the sense of pragmatism and practicality in the Saudi state which is also reflected in the conduct of its foreign policy. The Kingdom is inherently a conservative state. This is a function of its culture and history. It seeks to live in a world of peace and stability, and not to reshape the world in its image. Its pragmatic and practical approach is found in its dealings with the Arab, Muslim, and industrial states, as it is found in the world energy markets. The need to differentiate between a mirage and the real thing is as important for survival in the desert as it is in the real world.

A guiding principle of Saudi foreign policy is its commitment to peace and stability. Peace is a basic requirement of our Islamic faith. Islam, like Christianity and Judaism, prohibits acts of violence and commends the search for peace. In the words of God Almighty as revealed to the Prophet Mohammed: "if the enemy inclines towards peace, do thou also incline towards peace and trust in God." The achievement of peace requires the replacement of war and destruction with cooperation among nations and people. If the material of a new international order promises a new world where war would be rendered obsolete, the Saudi state must be reckoned among that order's principle enthusiasts. We have no vision of conquest beyond our borders, no foreign ventures beckon us. The sanctity of borders, the rule of law among nations; these are the corner-stones of the Saudi state's foreign policy.

In the Arab world, which represents the neighborhood we live in, the Kingdom strives to create an environment of peace and stability. Saudi Arabia has often acted as a mediator in inter-Arab disputes and lends its weight to the goal of achieving a just and lasting peace with Israel. Historically, it has also been one of the largest contributors of foreign aid to developing countries in general and Arab countries in particular.

The Kingdom is not a solitary country; the birthplace of Islam, and the guardian of its two holiest mosques, it has an obligation to over one billion Muslims world-wide. It is a founding member of the Organization of Islamic States and plays an active role in the Muslim world, whether to support Muslims fighting aggression in Afghanistan or in Bosnia, or by offering humanitarian assistance in Somalia or in Bangladesh.

As the country possessing the largest oil reserves in the world, the Kingdom is aware of its obligation to the rest of the globe to provide a stable supply of the commodity responsible for fueling the engines of economic growth world-wide. The Kingdom is committed to pursuing an energy policy based on "mutual security," that is, security of supply as well as security of demand. At the height of the Gulf Crisis, the Kingdom, against all odds, was able to increase its oil production from 5.5 million barrels per day to over 8 million barrels per day to assure stability in the oil markets. It lived up to the responsibility resting upon its shoulders as the world's major oil exporter. Only when the world is assured of stable, moderately-priced energy can it experience steady economic growth. This supply-demand relationship must be guided by free-market principles and not be influenced by artificial barriers.

The Kingdom is also committed to protecting the world's environment to assure future generations a safe and clean world. As inhabitants of the desert, Saudis are keenly aware of the natural link between people and their environment. It is for these reasons that environmental and safety standards in the Kingdom are among the highest in the world.

Saudi Arabia is one of the champions of the new world order characterized by collective action, under a United Nations' umbrella, to reverse aggression or promote humanitarian objectives. After all, it was in Saudi Arabia that the new world order was first tested, and its success there spurs us to promote it in other parts of the world. The Kingdom is convinced that when swords are turned into plowshares, and cooperation replaces competition among nations, peace and stability will reign throughout the world. Mankind will then be able to secure a future in which the nightmare of war, the horrors of destruction, the dangers of pollution, the effects of underdevelopment, and the pains of displacement vanish.

Conclusion

Winston Churchill once described the Kremlin as "a riddle wrapped in a mystery inside an enigma." Some modern-day observers have characterized the Kingdom in similar terms. The dearth of published literature on the Kingdom prior to 1970 was replaced by an explosion of works by instant experts who have sprung up from virtually nowhere. Their works have mostly dealt with the size of the country's oil fields, the veil of its women, the size of its airports, its arms purchases, and its potential instability. Very often, these studies have looked at the Kingdom from an ethnocentric perspective and concluded that because the Kingdom is "different from us," it must not be as good as we are. The world today is moving towards a global community in which interaction among different people and cultures is increasing and in which each must accept the others as they are rather than try to reshape them in one's own image.

Don't fall under the tyranny of forms when you look at Saudi Arabia. We are a monarchy to be sure. We don't have the forms of Western democracy; we have our own forms, and those issue from our own soil and traditions. We have our own checks and balances. Our Kings are not absolute monarchs, they work within a system of accountability that acknowledges the role of men of religion, the merchant and business class, the technocrats, and the tribal associations in a vast realm of some two million square kilometers in landmass.

I have tried to give you a short synopsis of the Saudi state, its origins and people. It is my hope that I have been able to portray the Kingdom and its people as they truly are — a state and people challenged by the requirements of the times, committed to meeting these challenges, together, without sacrificing their traditions and heritage. A state and people committed to promoting peace and stability at home and abroad. A state and people secure in their faith and in their destiny.

King Fahd

The Unification of the Arabian Peninsula: Background to the Formation of the Saudi Kingdom

by
Sheila Scoville

The Arabian Peninsula is part of the first cradle of civilization. The Semitic heritage of the Saudi Arabs reaches back nineteen centuries before the advent of Islam to the early Canaanites, who found refuge in the north of Arabia, to the Philistines who settled in Palestine, to the tribes of the Fertile Crescent in Mesopotamia, and to the peoples of Edan in Yemen. But since that early point in human history, the peninsula has been united only a few times. In fact, the area that is now Saudi Arabia may only have been united twice, once under the leadership of the Prophet Mohammed, and under the leadership of the Al-Saud family. After briefly discussing the shared history of the Semitic peoples, this article examines the unification of the Arabian Peninsula under the rule of Abdulaziz bin al-Saud.

It was through trade that the sedentary inhabitants of the Arabian peninsula came into contact with the great tribal leaders of the ancient pre-Christian and pre-Islamic eras. A millennium before Jesus, for example, the Nabateans of Petra, Madain Saleh, and al-Ula managed trading routes extending from modern Jordan throughout the Hijaz and into the Indian subcontinent and Pakistan. The ethics and values of the Semitic tribes, dependent as they were on the socio-economic traditions of the caravan, usually revolved around patriarchal allegiances. In the interior of Arabia, each tribal grouping was usually led by an elected "sheikh" who represented the communitys' interests in internal and external political affairs. The sheikh was also responsible for providing hospitality to the bedouin caravans that constantly moved from the south and eastern coasts of Arabia to the northern and far eastern markets. Contact with caravan traders from many ethnic backgrounds added to the richness of Arab culture.

The social ethic of the community centered around maintaining cohesion in the *qabilah* or the tribal confederations that kept relative peace between nomads and settlers. Tribal codes of honor and traditions were inherited; these involved keeping allegiance to extended kin and allies, and protecting the honor of the tribe against insults and military incursions. Tribal raiding, for which the region's people are famous, was regarded as a means of redistributing necessary commodities during hard economic times. During periods when severe draughts had destroyed pastures and wells, for example, raids were undertaken to replenish food and supplies. But even in the worst economic climate, raids would only be carried out against tribal caravans where a blood debt was owed.

In the early Christian but pre-Islamic era, the tribes of Arabia remained relatively untouched by the warring Byzantine and Persian Empires. Because of the Arab's reputation as keen desert warriors, and because of their relative geographical isolation, the tribes of the Arabian peninsula operated with autonomy throughout this period, and indeed through most of history. Few Arab tribes, for example, believed in either the Byzantine state's Christian traditions or the Persian state's Zoroastrian rituals. Instead, the Arabs' religious traditions varied widely by tribe, most of which worshipped idols as gods. Many tribes located their gods at the Ka'aba in Mecca, which they believed to be the house of Abraham. The *qabilah* had made the Ka'aba a central place where wide varieties of religious rituals could take place without political interference.

The first force that unified the Arabian peninsula was the advent of Islam: most of the region's tribes pledged allegiance to Mohammed and the revelations he had received from God. After years of exile and political persecution, Mohammed established himself in Medina as an arbitrator and civil servant. His fame and power grew quickly, and within a few years he and his followers were able to reclaim the Ka'aba as the focal site for Muslim worship. His influence spread through the Arab region.

Following Mohammed's death in 632 A.D., some tribes reverted to their pre-Islamic social patterns, but most gave their patronage to the four "rightly-guided" caliphs, Abu-Bakr, Umar, Uthman, and Ali. The religion began to split into factions, however, and after many intellectual and military skirmishes between Arab and Persian forces, the Sunni tradition was established in Arabia and the Shi'ite tradition was codified in Persia and eastern Iraq. The Arab leadership moved to Damascus during the Ummyad period, and then to Baghdad in the longer-lasting Abbasid Empire, in the eighth century. The Abbasids fell to the Mongol invasions in the thirteenth century, and by the sixteenth century leadership of the Sunni Islamic community was claimed by the Ottoman sultans in Istanbul.

The first Saudi movement took place in Arabia in 1744. In this period Saudi rulers controled an area roughly the size of Saudi Arabia today. Their forces were not sufficient, however, to match the onslaught of the armies of Mohammed Ali of Egypt, and the the first Saudi State was broken in 1818.

Two movements coinciede in the mid-ninteenth century, the resurgence of Moslem principles and the rise of a second Saudi action in the Nadj. Many people in the Nadj, the area surrounding Islam's two holy cities Mecca and Medina, had returned to the traditions of the pre-Islamic "Age of Ignorance (*jahiliya*)." One of the region's more charismatic holy men, Mohammed Abd al-Wahhab, began to organize a movement that wished to return the Muslim polity to fundamental interpretations of Qur'anic verses. He joined with Mohammed Abdulaziz Al-Saud, the head of an important family in the small town of Dar'iyya, to form a new community of Muslims. Their combined political and religious leadership proved to be influential, and provided the basis for a centralized authority that had been absent in central Arabia. Moreover, Saud's political savvy enabled the "Wahhabi" movement to expand throughout the region and eventually to control the two holy mosques. As the movement became stronger, however, it was seen as a threat by the Ottoman rulers. As the official protector of the Holy Cities, the Ottoman Sultanate wanted to control Arabia, and the second Saudi movement was stopped by his military forces in 1891.

In the early twentieth century, the Wahhabis found new leadership in another member of the Saudi clan, Abdulaziz bin Saud, who had reestablished his family's control over Dar'iyya and Riyadh in 1902. As a boy Abdulaziz had been forced to flee the Nadj region with his father, taking refuge in Kuwait because of threats made by the Ottoman military. A charismatic leader, he had mustered enough forces by age twenty-one to retake Riyadh for his tribe. By 1906 he was serving as emir of Najd and in 1913 he took control of Al-Hasa. His forces took the Hijaz in 1926, and in 1932 the Kingdom of Saudi Arabia was officially recognized as a sovereign nation.

The driving force behind his movement was the Wahhabi creed, and he proclaimed his intent to establish an Islamic State under the motto, "There is no God but God and Mohammed is his Prophet." In order to reestablish a Saudi-led Islamic State, Abdulaziz developed a policy that created an *ikhwan* or religious committees in the Kingdom to help people practice Islam in their daily lives. By redirecting peoples' commitments away from tribal allegiances and back to an Islamic focus, these committees helped to dissolve the old tribal spheres of influence and redefined people's allegiances to a central authority, something nomadic peoples had long rejected. Moreover, these committees brought Islam into the shops of artisans, craftsmen, and farmers so that they began to do their jobs with a new commitment to the Islamic good. Thus, Islam entered the twentieth century as a modern dynamic force.

As recognized as "Protector of the Haramain," King Abdulaziz found himself confronted by various outside forces in the early 1900s. During World War I, the Hashemi of Jordan joined forces with the British to defeat the secularized "Young Turk" regime in Istanbul. In a movement known in the West as the Arab Revolt, popularized by T.E. Lawrence's book *The Seven Pillars of Wisdom*, the Saudi sheikhs's came into close contact with British and other foreign advisors. However, recent scholarship has shown that the British were a major impediment to the Arab nationalist movement. Simultaneous uprisings in Syria and the Hijaz, for example, were stifled by British command, and Arab efforts to liberate Jordan and Syria prior to Britain's military advance into Sinai and Palestine were constantly foiled by the British and the French, since both countries wanted to make Arab lands colonial spheres of influence. Only after Jerusalem was taken in late 1917 by the British General Lord Allenby were the Arab forces encouraged to liberate territory, although still under the command of the Anglo-French Political Commission.[1]

The new Arab nation-states, created out of lands formerly held by the Ottoman Empire, were forged under a system of mandates established by the League of Nations, based on Woodrow Wilson's fourteen-point plan on establishing self-rule by indigenous peoples. Contrary to this plan, however, the British and French implemented a contract signed in 1916 to maintain effective control in the region. Many negotiators also felt that the Balfour Declaration calling for a Zionist state in Palestine should be supported.

The Saudi saw these states as colonialist and therefore unrepresentative of Arab and/or Islamic interests. In response, they rejected attempts by the British to engage in a colonialist dialogue. Through diplomacy, formal treaties outlining boundaries with the Arab rulers of the new nation states were established. These boundaries were formalized at the signing of the Treaty of Ugair in 1921.

During the period between the two World Wars, King Abdulaziz established relations with American oil companies wanting to explore the Kingdom for oil. He felt that American interests were commercial, not imperialist, and that American companies would be more likely to share industry and technology with the Saudi peoples. The War had also been expensive for the Kingdom, with negative effects on the country's agriculturally-based economy. Oil revenues would help alleviate these problems.

In 1945, King Abdulaziz and President Franklin Roosevelt met aboard an American battleship to begin diplomatic ties between Saudi Arabia and the United States. Prior to this meeting diplomatic relations between the two countries had been carried out by Aramco executives. The importance of this meeting was underlined by the fact that the trip marked King Abdulaziz's first trip outside the Kingdom. President Roosevelt's visit was shortly followed by a visit of Prime Minister Winston Churchill. Both leaders' discussions revolved around concerns over the situation in Palestine and about ways to avoid armed conflicts between Arabs and Israelis.

King Abdulaziz died in 1953, and his son Saud was elected by a council of sheikhs to assume leadership of the Kingdom. Since his death, five of his sons, Saud, Faisal, Khaled, and Fahd have ruled in his succession. Although it was Abudulaziz's vision that was able to unify most of the Arabian peninsula, he could hardly have foreseen that Saudi Arabia would some day be one of the

King Abdulaziz meets with U.S. President Franklin Roosevelt in 1945 to help forge strong diplomatic ties in the post-World War II era.

richest countries in the world. The modernization brought about by oil revenues has required many Saudis to redefine their positions in the community and in the world. Saudi Arabia is no longer an isolated Kingdom, but a key player in the global economy. Still, King Abdulaziz's vision of Saudi Arabia as a modern state free from colonial influence, based on the precepts of Wahhabi Islamic traditions, lives on in Saudi Arabia's government and society today.

Notes
1. Shiela A. Scoville, British Logistical Support to the Hashemites, Taif to Maan, 1916-1918, Ph.D. diss , U California at Los Angeles, 1982.

More Than Petroleum: A Diversified Economy

by
J. W. Wright, Jr.

The Saudi Arabian economy is one of the most complicated economies in the world. The discovery of oil in the 1920s set the Kingdom on an extremely rapid course toward modernization. Few societies have witnessed such accelerated economic growth as that caused by the infrastructure construction and chattel procurement that occurred from 1970 to 1985, when the first three Development Plans allocated over half of total government disbursements for infrastructure projects. During this period the Kingdom built ports and airports that are among the largest in the world, road and transportation systems that are comprehensive, and an industrial base that places the country far beyond an oil economy. In the 1990s, the government continues to support initiatives leading to institutional, legal, and regulatory maturation.

Consequently, the Kingdom has faced a number of unique development problems. Saudi Arabia has become, for example, the world's premier rentier state as it is highly dependent on the importation of foreign labour. Therefore, a major goal of each of the Saudi Arabian government's Five Year Development Plans has been the evolution of a domestic human resource pool that will decrease the Kingdom's dependency on foreign personnel and problems associated with their presence and facilitate the transfer of technology to the private and public sectors. Other development problems are exhibited in the sectors of finance, agriculture, and services. Government incentives almost entirely finance business expansion. Some claim liberal financing programs are a conduit through which oil revenues are redistributed to the population, while others claim these policies link business revenues and asset values more closely to aid and grant programs than to corporate efficiency. In agriculture, the Kingdom has become a net exporter of food products, but the cost in terms of water resource usage is severe. The service sector in Saudi Arabia seems to play an inordinately high role in the Kingdom's gross national product.

Reading the Saudi Arabian economy is definitely a complicated matter. Western advisors are often perplexed when traditional Keynsian-, Ricardian-, or Robertsonian-type models for modernization simply do not work in Saudi Arabia, and, for that matter, in the Arab Middle East. The Kingdom's culture and factors of endowment make its economy anomalous to Western notions about development. Moreover, numerous traditional industries in Saudi Arabia and barter-system ethics have not lent themselves easily to modernization, and ancient traditions in Arab culture tend to promote a service-oriented mercantilist hierarchy.

In my lecture today, following a brief discussion of the country's post World War II oil economy, I will look at each of the Five Year Development Plans and explain how they reflect significant levels of diversity in Saudi Arabia's economy. I will begin by looking at the Saudi Arabian economy in the 1940s, 1950s, and 1960s to establish the initial effects of the discovery of oil on the Kingdom. I will then look at the contents of each of the Five Year Development Plans and how they encouraged commercial diversification in the Kingdom. Of particular interest is the cycle of industrialization and how that cycle reflects a growing level of planning sophistication.

The Initiation of an Oil Economy

Saudi Arabia without oil would be a very different place. The mainstrean production of oil in the 1940s changed the complexion of the Kingdom's government, its industry, and its role in the Arab region's economic structure. With the coming of oil production came the intrusion of Western industry. These foreign companies created many of the successes that the Saudis claim to be their own, but the oil companies' ambitions in world oil markets often left them little time to consider the development of local economies. The Arab-American Oil Company (Aramco), although certainly more benevolent than most of its British counterparts, exerted extreme influence on the Monarchy and operated as a monopoly oil producer in Saudi Arabia in 1954.[1] The company dominated the Kingdom's political affairs until King Faisal issued edicts concerning the Saudization of the country's banking and oil industries.[2]

What the Saudi monarchy has always realized, however, is the power of oil. The increasing use of oil in the world's industrial production placed Saudi Arabia in a position of considerable international influence. In 1935 world oil consumption peaked at 1.8 million barrels of oil a day; by the end of World War II consumption had risen to 7.8 million barrels a day; and by 1957 it had reached 18.3 million barrels a day[3] The Middle East region was likewise dependent on oil consumption. In 1954 sixty-nine percent of total energy consumption was oil based,[4] primarily because other natural resources were either non-existent or underdeveloped in the region.[5] At that time, seventy percent of the world's known oil reserves were in Iraq, Kuwait, and Saudi Arabia (Saudi Arabia holding the lion's share of reserves.[6] Consequently, oil production and petroleum revenues rose dramatically in the post-war period, as is shown in Table One below. Oil fields were completed in Qatif and Ain Dar in 1945, with combined production of 170,000 barrels a day. Similar wells were opened throughout the country's eastern region, and the first off-shore well was opened at Safaniya in 1951. By 1953 one hundred and thirty-seven wells produced 845,000 barrels of oil daily. In 1954, the refinery at Ras Tanura, which in 1944 had a 50,000 barrel a day capacity, was expanded so that it could process two million barrels a day.[7]

Saudi Arabian Oil Production and Petroleum Revenues, 1944-1954

Year	Production (barrels)	Oil Refined in Country (barrel)	Saudi Gov'ts Oil Revenue ($US)
1945	21,311,000	2,953,623	4,820,000
1946	59,944,000	29,297,101	13,500,000
1947	89,852,000	39,065,060	20,380,000
1948	142,853,000	45,086,139	31,860,000
1949	174,009,000	46,269,619	66,000,000
1950	199,547,000	38,364,333	112,000,000
1951	277,963,000	58,107,534	155,000,000
1952	301,861,000	62,204,161	212,000,000
1953	308,294,000	74,559,673	166,000,000
1954	347,000,000	79,800,000	260,000,000

During the 1950s and throughout the 1960s, Saudi Arabia operated as an oil economy with few other sectors producing products for export. In 1953, 90.3 percent of government income came from oil taxes and sales. Saudi government revenues from oil sales continued to increase to $340 million in 1960, to $663 million in 1965, to $1.2 billion in 1970. By 1973 the refinery at Ras Tanura had the capacity to load 439,000 barrels of oil per hour, nearly ten times the amount that could be refined twenty years earlier.[8]

In the 1960s, however, the Saudi government became concerned with the concentration of the Kingdom's industrial base.[9] It was also concerned about meeting the increasing needs in the local market for refined oil. Demand for refined petroleum had grown at an annual rate of nearly fourteen percent in the Middle East,[10] and at a rate of twenty-seven percent in Saudi Arabia since 1950.[11] The increased use of the Suez Canal by oil tankers also indicated a need to find more effective ways to transport oil to ports on the Red Sea. In response to these developments, expansion of refining capacity at Ras Tanura continued and the Trans-Arabian pipeline was built to carry oil from Saudi's Eastern Province to the Mediterranean shores near Sidon. The pipeline was completed in September 25, 1950,[12] and by December it carried oil equivalent in quantity to that of seventy-two oil tanker runs through the Suez Canal.[13]

Still, the Kingdom needed new ports with industrial capacity on both coasts. The fact that two pipelines were being built through Iraq[14] and that plans to expand the Suez canal were under way, threatened Saudi's strategic position in the West. Moreover, the threat of war could not be ignored. If the

Suez Canal were to close, or if the pipeline were to be destroyed, Saudi Arabia's revenues from shipments through the western region could be decimated. Simultaneously, in the eastern region, the need for new ports was exacerbated by higher demand for oil from Asian nations.

The Roots of Economic Development Planning

From 1950 to 1964, oil revenues provided the government with ninety percent of its total revenues,[15] and the remaining ten percent came from agricultural production and caravan trade.[16] While sales of crude oil may have provided the capital needed to finance economic development, it was planned restructuring that paved the way for the emergence of rapid development,[17] which generated increases in real wealth during the 1970s.[18] King Faisal's accession to the throne in 1964 brought a new Saudi goverment attitude about development planning. He believed major offensives were needed to develop a "dual economy"[19] whereby the Kingdom could 1) regain control of its natural resources, 2) exploit more effectively those resources for its own industrial development, and 3) support private sector development of traditional industries through small business development.[20]

Saudi Arabia planned to shake its dependence on foreign industrial intervention and become a member of the world's power elite in one generation.[21] Faisal's strategy was fivefold. First, government spending would be redirected toward projects that serve dual infrastructure and security functions, i.e. the construction of industrial grade roads, military-ready civilian airports, and state-of-the-art communications and medical systems. Second, government ministries and agencies would be established that could begin to regulate commercial activity in the Kingdom. Third, industrial construction would focus on oil refinement products, such as petro-chemicals, fertilizers, and lubricants. Fourth, government planners were to depend less on the advice of oil executives and more on the advice of hired consultants, namely the U. S. Corps of Engineers and the United States-Saudi Arabian Joint Commission for Economic Cooperation. Finally, beginning in 1966, mandates were made calling for a central agency to coordinate government planning, procurement, and spending.[22]

The effect of these directives was immediate. The percentage of government expenditures for development projects rose from seventeen percent in 1958 ($96.5 million)[23] to twenty-nine percent ($350 million) of total government expenditures in 1969. As a result, gross fixed capital formation in the non-oil sector rose at an 18.68 percent average annual pace between 1964 and 1969. Overall gross national product rose at eight percent annually.[24]

The function of consultants also changed dramatically. By the end of Faisal's reign, the U.S. Corp. of Engineers had become the dominant force in

Saudi Arabia's development planning efforts. The reason is not that Aramco had a negative influence on the country; indeed, Aramco had built the Kingdom's first school systems, health care facilities, and training programs *en gratis*.[25] Rather, strategic concerns that too many of the Kingdom's infrastructure and support systems were being commercially controlled took precedence. By working with the U.S. Corp., Saudi Government officials felt they could purchase a broader-based transfer of technology and that the Corps could better design and construct infrastructure facilities to serve civilian and security purposes.[26] The Corp also understood that non-military facilities such as radio and television stations were of vital interest to the Saudi government's stability, as well as to the development of educational and social programs.[27] In 1964, having just completed a commercially operative airbase in Dahran, the Corps began construction on major radio and television communication facilities in Jeddah and Riyadh.[28] The Corps took charge later of many civilian infrastructure projects including networks for airports (twenty-three), cellular communications,[29] manufacturing facilities, power generation plants, medical supplies, satellite telecommunications, training facilities and transportation.[30] The Corps' role was also supportive of Saudi security interests and of a planning process that was primarily concerned with private sector developments.[31]

Another development objective (or component of the 5-year strategy) was restructuring the Kingdom's oil industry. The predominate export at the time was crude oil, but some Saudi planners believed profit margins were being lost to the designs of foreign oil companies. Initiatives were taken to assure the sales of more refined oil products that carried higher price premiums on world commodity markets. As a result, spending for refinery expansion and petro-chemical development was significantly increased and the level of value-added oil products in the GDP rose at a higher rate than that of non-oil value-added products (traditional and handicraft products). The ratio of oil to non-oil products in value-added GDP is shown in the following table.[32] In the long-range this situation changed, as steps were taken to develop agriculture, cottage manufacturing, and industrial cities. But the first step was to harness the potential of oil.[33] In addition, the government began buying Aramco shares. By 1973, the Saudi government owned twenty-five percent of Aramco's shares, by 1976 sixty percent and by 1980 100 percent.[34]

Value-added GDP, 1965-1970

Year	Total	Non-oil	Oil	% of Va-oil GDP
1965	10,258	7,297	2,961	28.87
1966	11,976	7,457	4,519	37.74
1967	13,843	7,712	6,131	44.29
1968	14,657	7,764	6,893	47.03
1969	15,974	8,705	7,270	45.51
1970	17,399	9,293	8,106	46.59

Faisal's next objective was to strengthen the government's control of the planning, policy and regulatory processes. The Kingdom's first efforts at planning came in 1958 with the establishment of the Economic Development Committee, which was replaced with the Supreme Planning Board in 1960.[35] However, it was not until this Board was replaced by the Central Planning Organization in 1965 (currently the Ministry of Planning), that fully integrated budgets and development plans were published regularly. The plans written between 1966 and 1970 are the precursors of the often-quoted and highly successful Five Year Development Plans, which began in 1970.[36] As a result of these plans, oil revenues fueled development programs and propelled the country's transition into a modern industrial society.[37]

The government's interest in institutional development should also be emphasized. One of the more striking examples of institutional maturation during the era of King Faisal is found in the financial sector. Six banks operated in the Kingdom prior the establishment of the Saudi Arabian Monetary Agency in 1952: the Netherlands Trading Company, Banque de l'Indochina, Bank of Palestine, National Bank of Pakistan, British Bank of the Middle East, and the Egyptian Bank.[38] The Saudi owned National Bank of Commerce was the first Saudi bank, approved by the King in 1952.[39] The second, Bank of Riyadh, was licensed by the Al-Suwailim, the Abu Dawoud, and Bin-Zagr families in 1957. Neither the foreign banks nor the two Saudi run banks were registered with the government, although the Netherlands Trading Company did serve as the holder of the Saudi government's foreign currencies.[40]

In general, foreign banks provided limited banking services to the Western guest worker community and to foreign Muslims visiting the holy cities of Mecca and Medina. The Saudi Arabian Monetary Agency (SAMA) was created in 1952 to function as a licensing bureau, gold and silver changer, holder of the government's monetary reserves, and regulator of banks operating in the Kingdom.[41] As suggested by the U.S. Federal Reserve Board in its consulting reports written in 1951, SAMA was founded as a semi-autonomous government corporation. It did not have authority to print money or to handle a local currency until 1959, and had little control over the country's financial system until the mid-1960s.[42]

Under the leadership of King Faisal Saudi Arabia began to bring the Saudi financial system under its control. The impetus for many regulations came from the near failure of the Bank of Riyadh in 1964. SAMA intervened by buying a thirty-eight percent stake in the bank. In an effort to avert further bank failures, SAMA's powers were significantly expanded in 1965. In 1966 the Banking Control Code was issued which significantly constrained and standardized the operations of banks in the Kingdom.[43] As a result of this standardization, the licensing of banks grew rapidly in the late 1960s and the early 1970s.

By the time Crown Prince Khalid became King in 1975, there were fourteen Western-styled banks operating in the country. In addition, a number of specialized banks were created under Faisal to improve the distribution of funds earmarked for development. The Saudi Arabian Agricultural Bank was founded in 1964; the Public Investment Fund was chartered in 1971; and the Saudi Credit Assistance Bank Act was signed in 1973. The Saudi Industrial Development Bank was established in 1974 with objectives of providing medium and long-term loans for up to fifty percent of the total requirements of new industrial construction, expansion, modernization and renovation projects. The Fund had a particular interest in industrial infrastructure projects such as private electrical companies, concrete factories, desalination plants and electricity generation facilities. The Real Estate Development Fund (REDF) also made its first loans in 1974, intent on solving real estate shortages in private and public housing. The Saudi Fund for Development allowed the government to participate in external financing opportunities.[44]

King Faisal's planning model also included a comprehensive training component, which was in the directives he gave to the United States-Saudi Arabia Joint Commission for Economic Cooperation when it was founded in 1972. By providing consulting services to the Kingdom's industries and institutions, the Joint Economic Commission was made responsible for organizing cooperative efforts in the fields of accounting, agricultural banking, demographic planning, industrial construction, labour training, scientific research and water management. The Commission was unique both in format and influence as it focused almost entirely on government employees.[45] In essence, the development of Saudi Arabia's economic and financial systems is based on King Faisal's madates toward development planning. This means that Saudi Arabia's current economic system has developed in less than thirty years; the progress made in this short period of time is impressive. I will look next at the

direction of planning and development finance in each of the Five-Year
Development Plans.

An Analysis and Description of the Five Five-Year Development Plans

The formal publication of five-year development plans began in 1970 with
a plan that paled in the face of economic conditions in the aftermath of the
1973 Arab-Israeli war. The OPEC oil embargo had changed the structure of
world oil markets dramatically and significantly elevated Saudi Arabia's position in the international economic strata. The oil revenues that followed in
1974 dwarfed any expectations that had been written into the original plan,
rising from $2,744 and $4,340 million in 1972 and 1973, to $22,574 and $25,676
million in 1974 and 1975.[46] During the pre-plan period (1965-1970) expenditures were only 24,800 million riyals.

King Khaled did not inherit a failed planning system, but rather, a system
that had derived great benefit from the experience of writing a national planning effort,[47] and he had at his disposal King Faisal's network of development-
financing institutions. More importantly, the first plan placed the Kingdom on
a three-pronged strategy that guided the second and third plans: 1) the diversification of the economic structure through growth in manufacturing, 2) the
short-term mobilization of foreign human resources and the long-term training of an indigenous work force, and 3) the expansion of oil-related businesses. Social welfare facilities and incentives for private enterprise were given
much emphasis. Projected expenditures for the first, second and third plans
were as follows:

Financial Appropriation for the First Five-Year Development Plan
1970-1975 (million Saudi Riyals, constant 1970 prices)

Appropriations	Amount	Percentage
Administration	7,717.4	18.6
Defense	9,555.0	23.1
Human Resource	7,377.7	17.8
Health and Social Affairs	1,,921.1	4.7
Public Utilities	4572.3	11.1
Transport and Comm.	7,474.5	18.1
Industrial Construction	1,098.5	2.7
Agriculture	1,467.7	3.6
Trade and Services	127.3	0.3
Total	41,313.5	100.0[48]

Financial Appropriation for the Second Five-Year Development Plan
1975-1980 (million Saudi Riyals, constant 1970 prices)

Appropriations	Amount	Percentage
Administration	38,179	7.7
Defense	78,196	15.7
Human Resource	80,124	16.1
Health and Social Affairs	33,213	6.7
Infrastructure Development	112,945	22.7
Agriculture	2,900	2.3
Economic Resources Dev.	92,135	18.5
Other	60,578	10.3
Total	498,270	100.0

Financial Appropriation for the Third Five-Year Development Plan
1975-1980 (million Saudi Riyals, constant 1970 prices) [49]

Appropriations	Amount	Percentage
Administration	3,1400	4.0
Defense		(not listed separately)
Human Resource	129,600	16.6
Health and Social Affairs	61,200	7.8
Infrastructure Development	249,100	31.8
Agriculture	2,270	2.9
Economic Resources Dev.	261,800	33.4
Other	47,330	3.5
Total	782,700	100.0

It is clear that the goal of the first plan was to raise the general standard of living through infrastructure development. Next to expenditures on defense and administration, the country's road and communications systems received high priority. Many of the defense expenditures went to facilities that served dual civilian and military functions. Human resource expenditures were the next priority, followed by the development of a public utility system. Agriculture was not as yet a priority. Given the turbulent years in which it operated, and the changing of leadership in the Kingdom, the first plan was surprisingly successful in constructing infrastructure.[50]

The oil price hikes in 1974 allowed the government to attack infrastructure problems more aggressively in the second plan, which operated on a budget six times that of the first plan. The percentages of total expenditures set in the first plan for the development of human resources and health and social development did not change substantially. Defense expenditures, while increased significantly in dollar amount, declined as a percentage of expenditures. The "Other" account consists of external assistance, emergency funds, and reserves. During this period a number of social welfare goals were reached, including the provision of free medical services, subsidized housing, and the offering of expense-free education and training.

What is most obvious is the increase in infrastructure expenditures in the second plan. Including spending for economic resource development-the construction of resource-related product processing facilities (agriculture, mining, natural gas)-physical construction for industry represents over forty percent of the budget. Add to this the amount of military construction and the level of loans made for agricultural development and sixty-five percent of funding directed into real estate intensive projects. These expenditures clearly represent a continuation of King Faisal's initiative to create a broader oil-related industrial base while supporting non-oil production.

King Khalid's objective was to intensify efforts toward manufacturing diversification. At the heart of these efforts was the creation of industrial cities at Yanbu and Jubail. Both cities are based near major refining facilities where natural gas, which had previously been lost when oil was extracted, was gathered and used to fuel the manufacture of hydrocarbons and petrochemicals. Included in the plans were oil-related plants capable of producing fertilizers, methanol, ethylene, polyethylene, ethylene glycol, butane, liquified gas, plastics and sulfur. Non-oil related production facilities were planned for aluminum, beverages, cement, food processing, electric consumer goods, tires and vehicles.

As the second plan unfolded, structural developments began to reflect King Khalid's objectives. As the following table illustrates, all sectors increased their output during the 1975-1980 period, but the infrastructure and manufacturing sectors far outperformed the more traditional sectors. The construction sector's share of non-oil GDP doubled. In addition, there was a strong movement away from employment in agriculture, with some fifteen percent of the labor force leaving agriculture and moving into jobs in the manufacturing sector.[51] The non-oil sector increased dramatically from less than two percent in 1963 to 27.4 percent in 1973, and 33.9 percent in 1980. Non-oil sector growth tripled oil sector growth.

The third plan represented a basic continuation of the objectives set forth in the first and second plans, including a major emphasis on infrastructure and resource development. Funding for expansion in these two sectors was raised by 149 percent to a combined total expenditure of 510 billion riyals. Continuing emphasis was placed on the building of facilities that could be used for defense and civilian purposes, although it was more specific in promoting growth in the non-oil sectors. Construction of ports and airports was de-emphasized as more attention was paid to building industrial facilities. This was evident to an even greater extent after Crown Prince Fahd became King in 1982.

As the mandates of the third plan were implemented, distinct structural changes became apparent. The construction industry declined as a percentage of non-oil sector growth, while non-oil manufacturing rose from five percent to seven percent. More importantly, the service sector took on a somewhat new identity, gaining sixty-four percent of the economy's output in 1985. With road and port facility expansion nearing completion by 1985, the transportation sector saw significant growth, as did commercial trade (wholesaling and retailing), and the real estate trade established itself as a viable industry. Predictably, the service and manufactuing sectors became the big winners in terms of employment transfer, with another ten percent of the workforce moving into non-agricultural jobs.

Sectoral Share of Non-oil GDP[52]

Annual Percentage Growth Rate of Real Output

Sector	1975/1980	1980/1985
Producing Sector		
Agriculture	5.1	6.2
Mining	4.6	-16.5
Manufacturing	9.8	6.9
Utilities	21.9	18.6
Construction	15.8	-0.9
Sub-total	6.9	-7.2
Service Sector		
Trade	22.7	9.2
Transport	19.3	7.1
Finance	14.0	4.4
Other Services	3.3	1.9
Government	—	6.4
Subtotal	15.1	6.9
Total non-oil Sector	14.8	6.4
Oil Sector	4.8	-14.2

Gross Domestic Product by Sector, 1973-1980

Share of GDP

	Share of GDP 1973, %	Share of GDP 1975, %	Share of GDP 1980, %	Share of GDP 1985, %	Share of GDP 1990,%
Producing Sectors					
Agriculture	1.0	0.9	5.4	4.1	4.8
Mining	0.2	0.4	1.0	1.1	1.1
Manufacturing	1.4	1.9	4.8	7.3	10.4
Petrochemicals	—	—	—	—	2.6
Utilities	—	0.1	0.2	0.5	0.5
Construction	8.4	12.9	32.3	23.5	17.7
Sub total	11.0	16.2	41.8	36.5	37.1
Service Sector					
Trade	2.7	4.9	13.2	15.8	15.5
Transport	3.2	5.6	11.8	13.0	14.3
Real Estate	—	—	8.0	7.1	6.2
Finance	2.9	3.7	3.4	5.0	6.6
Other Services	1.1	1.5	3.9	4.5	4.6
Government	6.5	5.9	17.5	18.1	15.7
Subtotal	16.4	21.6	58.2	63.5	62.9
Total non-oil sector	27.4	37.8	34.8	60.2	57.1
Total oil sector	72.6	62.2	65.2	39.8	42.9
Total	100.0	100.0	100.0	100.0	100.0

Three main sets of structural changes became apparent.[53] First the level of growth in the economy was being driven by or was concentrated in manufacturing and services. However, it must also be noted that the demand for consumption in the non-oil sectors is directly tied to government financing and procurement programs. Up to seventy-five percent of private sector spending is supported by government financed assistance, grant, loan, or subsidy programs. While the non-oil sectors were becoming more efficient, and were therefore less directly affected by oil sales, these sectors were still very much affected indirectly when government financing programs went into retrenchment.[54]

The second structural change was manifested in the interaction between the various sectors of the economy, especially in the traditional sectors. By the beginning of the fourth plan, Saudi Arabia became a grain exporter. At the same time, employment in agriculture declined by twenty-five percent, while the service sector accounted for seventy-three percent of the Kingdom's patriot employment.[55] The redistribution of employment by sector is illustrated in the following table.

Employment by Economic Activity
1979-1980 and 1984-1985

| | 1979-1980 | | 1984-1985 | | Growth Rate |
	(Thousand)	(%)	(Thousand)	(%)	(%)
Producing Sectors	1,424.2	47.0	2,067.2	46.5	7.7
Agriculture	545.6	18.0	617.4	13.9	2.5
Other Mining	2.3	0.1	5.1	0.1	17.3
Other Manufacturing	170.4	5.6	411.4	9.3	19.3
Utilities	67.0	2.2	147.4	3.3	17.1
Construction	638.9	21.1	885.9	19.9	6.8
Service Sectors	1,157.7	38.3	1,844.6	41.5	9.8
Trade	323.1	10.76	556.1	12.5	11.5
Transport	180.0	6.0	303.4	6.8	11.0
Finance	51.8	1.7	136.3	3.1	21.4
Other Services	602.8	19.9	848.8	19.1	7.1
Government*	399.4	13.2	469.1	10.5	3.3
Subtotal:					
Non-Oil Sectors	2,981.3	98.5	4,380.9	98.5	8.0
Oil Sectors	44.7	1.5	65.1	1.5	7.8
Total	3,026.0	100.0	4,446.0	100.0	8.0

note: * Excludes noncivilian employment, and includes daily wage workers not classified as civil servants.

Third, with increased industrial diversification the direction of production changed from large industrial projects to small and medium sized manufacturers. With this trend a strong middle class political-economic element in the community developed in Saudi Arabia.[56] From a development point of view, economic reliance on this new business class will create significant finance gaps, but they also should create substantially more jobs. It is important to remember, though, that small businesses are riskier to operate, more difficult to finance, and studies show that there is a high level of managerial inefficiency among Saudi's entrepreneurial class.[57]

The fourth plan (1985-1990) marks a decided change in the Saudi government's position toward development.[58] As dramatically as oil prices rose in 1974, they plummeted in 1983-1984, leaving the government to face its first budget deficit in twenty years. Because infrastructure construction was ostensibly complete and most medium and large industrial firms had received liberal financing, it was decided that the private sector needed to be weaned away from the public sector.[59] As Looney puts it, "the basic messages of the (fourth) plan are that the state, having made massive investments in establishing a modern infrastructure, wants the private sector to shoulder more of the investment burden, and eventually to emerge as the main force in the economy."[60]

At the beginning of the fourth five-year plan, there were about two thousand producing entities in the Kingdom. Those firms supplied only fifty percent of the goods consumed even though the physical capacity to supply almost all of the Kingdom's consumer goods existed.[61] The crux of the problem lay in the fact that facilities were not being managed for maximum efficiency. Too often business owners could not distinguish between cash flow generated from profits and money received from government subsidies.[62] Imports had fallen twenty-eight precent during the third plan, and it was hoped that they would fall another thirty percent by 1990. Due to these conditions, the fourth plan emphasized the efficient use of the Kingdom's new facilities.[63] Planned overall growth during the period was only four percent. But growth in agriculture was placed at six percent, in the financial sector at nine percent, and in private sector manufacturing at 15.5 percent. The following table shows the actual growth rates by sector.

Sectoral Growth Rates(percent)

	1987	1988	1989	1990
Agriculture	15.4	12.1	11.3	9.0
Mining	3.3	-2.5	18.3	65.2
Oil and Gas	3.4	-2.6	18.7	66.7
Other Mining	-1.9	1.8	5.0	6.0
Manufacturing	10.9	3.7	15.5	11.0
Petroleum Refining	18.0	-2.3	15.5	11.0
Other Manufacturing	.9	8.0	7.1	7.5
Public Utilities	30.0	6.0	5.0	6.0
Construction	-2.3	-5.0	1.4	2.0
Financial and Business				
Services	2.9	9.2	7.1	-2.5
Defense	-2.0	3.2	4.8	10.0

Source: Ministry of Finance and National Economy, Kingdom of
         Saudi Arabia.

Unfortunately, oil revenues did not rebound as hoped, and budgeted spending did not take place as expected in either the third or the fourth plan. Even after the budget cuts, government spending remained consistent with the strategy underlying the plan. Allocation declined, with construction in both industry and infrastructure suffering the largest cuts. Spending on social services was maintained, and the government's committment to developing a more highly skilled indigenous work force kept funds for human resources in tact. These two areas of the budget seemed to be immune to cutbacks under the fourth plan. In terms of growth, the agriculture sector showed the most resiliance on a sectoral basis. The following three tables show intended and actual expenditures of the plan, and the fourth table shows sectoral growth rates from 1987-1990.

Development expenditures during the Fourth Plan

| | Expenditure structure | | |
| | Third Plan | | Fourth Plan |
	Plan	Actual	Plan
Spending category			
Economic resources development	31.3	21.4	26.1
Human resources development	21.3	22.2	27.1
Health and social services	10.0	12.4	17.9
Transport and communications	22.7	24.7	15.4
Municipalities and housing	14.7	19.3	13.5
Total: Development agencies	100.0%	100.0%	100.0%

	Expenditure level			
	Third Plan		Fourth Plan	
				Change from Third Plan
	Plan	Actual	Plan	Actual
Spending category				
Economic resources development	190.7	120.4	130.7	+ 8.6%
Human resources development	129.6	124.3	135.3	+ 8.8%
Health and social services	61.2	69.6	89.7	+ 28.9%
Transport and communications	138.6	139.1	76.9	-44.7%
Municipalities and housing	89.3	108.9	67.4	-38.1%
Total: Development agencies	609.4	562.3	500.0	-11.1%

Amounts are in current prices.
Source: Fourth Development Plan, p. 73.

Budget Allocations by Sector (1401/2-1408/9)

	1405/6	1407	1408/9
Human resource development	23,962	23,725	23,388
Transport and communications	16,500	11,934	9,493
Economic resource development	14,434	8,439	5,888
Health and social development	14,830	11,094	10,806
Infrastructure development	6,670	4,300	3,555
Municipal services	11,890	8,100	7,017
Public administration &,			
government utilities etc.	31,582	31,266	25,058
Lending to credit institutions*	9,300	3,590	590
Local subsidies	8,343	6,800	5,325
Non-defense expenditure	137,511	109,248	91,120
Defence and security	64,085	60,752	50,080
Total Planned expenditure (SRm)	201,596	170,000	141,200

*Includes transfer to Saudi Fund for Development.
Source: Various SAMA and government publications

The fifth plan has the same fundamental objectives as the fourth plan, although efforts toward education and training have obviously intensified. For the first time, human resource development receives the highest level of funding, 18.7 percent of the total budget and thirty-five percent of the non-government budget. This represents the government's intention to support the managerial needs of the private sector and the training needs of government agencies that are receiving additional regulatory power. It is also a call to move away from public sector dependence and to reward private sector activity.[64] The fact that the oil sector's proportionate contribution to GDP had fallen to twenty-five percent in 1991 put the burden of creating new employment opportunities more squarely on the shoulders of small and medium sized businesses. These firms still account for eighty percent of the Kingdom's total employment. In addition, banks are called upon to provide more medium and long-term financing to entrepreneurs and small manufacturers in support for the development process.

These components of the fifth plan are also part of a greater plan by King Fahd's government to replace foreign labor and management with Saudi personnel. The fourth plan called for replacing 600,000 non-national employees over the five year period and increasing the Saudi labor force by 370,000.[65]

Only about half of this amount was reached, and, consequently, the need for continued training of Saudi workers is probably the single most important issue facing the Kingdom in the 1990s. With the expected opening of 354,000 jobs from 1990-1995 for 754,000 new Saudi entrants to the workforce, the fifth plan only calls for the replacement of 220,400 foreign workers.

Finally, another current aim of the government is to operate with balanced budgets. The 1990s have thus far been turbulent years for Saudi Arabia, and highly volatile oil markets plus the costs of war have not made it easy for the government to meet this goal. The budget deficits of the 1980s can be resolved, however, by replacing public sector spending with private sector incentives.

Examples of Saudi Arabia's Development Planning Success

As a result of the planning efforts of Kings Faisal and Khaled, and due to the continued leadership of King Fahd, Saudi Arabia has moved rapidly into an era of modern development. Today established industrial cities stand in places that were once small villages. Goods are now regularly produced by Saudi companies that twenty years ago were considered luxuries. Education and health care are free to all citizens. The country's infrastructure and defense systems are second to none. And the country has successfully created a diversified economy.

The following tables illustrate how the Saudi economic landscape has grown since 1964, when nearly one hundred percent of the Kingdom's petroleum sales were in crude oil. All of the Kingdom's banks operate as joint ventures and operate under substantial regulation from the Saudi Arabian Monetary Agency. The number of factories will top three thousand by the end of the current five-year plan. Growth in the manufacturing and service sectors has redefined the Kingdom's employment activity. Product services have become the leading employer of all sectors, including government and military. Commercial trade has doubled employment opportunities offered to the public since 1970. Non-oil manufacturing has risen from three percent of total employment to 12.7 percent. Agriculture, the largest employer in 1970, has declined by twenty-five percent in terms of number of people employed. The number of construction jobs has fallen by nine percentage points, and employment in transportation is sixty percent lower today than it was twenty years ago. Agricultural production exceeds ten percent of non-oil GDP.

This does not mean that planning in the oil sector should be put into the background. Oil sales will continue to be the Kingdom's main source of revenue and foreign reserve, and oil-related projects will continue to have priority in the future. The country's new economic order does, however, lessen its dependency on one source of production and reduces the chance that sudden swings in oil prices could affect the economy as a whole. More importantly, the new Saudi economy has proven that tradition and transition are not misplaced polarities. "The case of Saudi Arabia shows that the traditional institution may indeed support rapid economic modernization,"[66] and it proves that Saudi Arabia is more than petroleum. It is a diversified economy.

Appendix:

Saudi Arabian Commercial Banks as of 1989
($ million)

Bank's Name	Total Assets	Loans	Equity	Profit(Loss)
National Commerical Bank	23,100.8	9,940.0	853.3	0.0
Riyad Bank	11,322.8	2,705.9	1,120.0	67.9
Saudi American Bank	7,078.6	1,757.8	514.6	112.5
al-Bank al-Saudi al-Fransi	4,807.2	1,381.5	293.9	27.5
al-Rajhi Banking and Investment Corporation	4,470.7	N/A	561.1	274.1
Arab National Bank	4,187.2	982.3	496.4	86.0
Saudi British Bank	3,351.0	732.0	191.2	32.9
al-Bank al-Saudi al-Hollandi	2,732.7	730.8	178.0	21.3
Saudi Cairo Bank	N/A	N/A	N/A	N/A
United Saudi Commerical Bank	1,377.8	258.7	85.4	25.5
Saudi Investment Bank	1,337.5	165.8	59.0	2.9
Bank al-Jazira	1,292.1	488.9	62.6	(19.8)

Source: Compiled from MEED (August) 1990 (34): 13; MEED (June) 1989 (35): 5.

Number of Factories, Capital, and
Labor in Saudi Arabia during 1982-1989

Year	Factories	%	Labor (Thousands)	%	Captial (SR Millions)	%
1982	1,670	10.9	53,851	9.4	109,919	10.6
1983	1,739	11.2	54,880	9.6	113,334	11.1
1984	1,785	11.5	55,431	9.7	117,360	11.5
1985	1,864	12.0	59,780	10.5	126,204	12.3
1986	2,028	13.1	59,780	10.5	126,204	12.3
1987	2,061	13.3	94,805	16.6	140,620	14.0
1988	2,138	13.8	95,563*	16.8	143,202	14.0
1989	2,199	14.2	96,199*	16.9	145,191	14.2

Source: Soufi, et al, 1991. Gross financing estimates—actual total capital not available.

A Summary of Employment Distribution
by Economic Activities for 1970-1990 (percentages)

Activity	1970	1975	1980	1985	1990
Manufacturing (including petroleum and refining) and other	5.4	3.0	4.0	9.3	12.7
Mining and quarrying and other (including oil, and natural gas)	2.3	3.0	2.6	1.6	2.5
Commerce and other * Sectors	8.3	13.0	14.3	15.8	15.0
**Product Services	1.4	1.3	1.2	22.2	22.9
Transport, Communications, and Storage	18.1	19.0	19.1	6.8	7.0
Social and Community Services includes Education and Health	4.7	5.5	8.2	—	—
Utilities	1.1	1.2	1.3	—	—
Subtotal	41.3	46.0	50.7	55.7	60.1
Public Administration	5.5	5.5	7.0	10.5	10.6
Construction	12.8	20.5	25.4	19.9	13.8
Agriculture, Forestry, and Fishing	40.4	28.0	16.9	13.9	15.5
Total	100.0	100.0	100.0	100.0	100.0

* Such as trade, restaurants, and hotels
** Such as insurance, real estate, and business services

Gross Domestic Product (Total, Non-oil and Agriculture)
1970-1989 (Million SR Current Prices)

| Development Plans | Year | Gross Domestic Product (GDP) | | | Agriculture | |
		Total	Non-Oil	Amount	% of Total	% of Total
	1970	19826	8050	1025	5.2	12.7
First	1971	25623	8857	1063	4.2	12.0
Plan	1972	34218	10398	1127	3.3	10.8
	1973	67420	13502	1218	1.8	9.0
	1974	120839	21764	1347	1.1	6.2
	1975	156048	38446	1529	1.0	4.0
Second	1976	191512	59688	1788	0.9	3.0
Plan	1977	222807	82208	3067	1.4	3.7
	1978	246241	102746	4193	1.7	4.1
	1979	341307	125075	4601	1.4	3.7
	1980	485879	152240	5398	1.1	3.6
Third	1981	539064	180394	6535	1.2	3.6
Plan	1982	462255	205662	8345	1.8	4.1
	1983	395817	215336	9645	2.4	4.5
	1984	351398	214869	11620	3.3	5.4
	1985	313941	216983	13789	4.4	6.5
Fourth	1986	271091	203630	15861	5.9	7.9
Plan	1987	275453	205010	18312	6.7	9.1
	1988	285145	215990	20895	7.3	10.1
	1989	N/A	N/A	N/A	N/A	N/A

Source: Ministry of Planning, 1990; SAMA, Statistical Summary 1990.
N/A= not available

Saudi Aramco's Projected
Long-term Expansion Program for the Years 1991-2003

1991-1994	Safaniya	Tie-in platforms	265
	North Hawiyah	(1) GOSP-2 and 3	160
	North Hawiyah	Water Injection Project	300
	Marjan	Completion	175
	Zuluf	(2) WCHF	320
1992-1995	South Hawiyah	GOSP-4	160
	South Hawiyah	Water Injection	150
	*N.A.	Sea-water Pump Station	100
	Uthmaniyah	GOSP-5	150
1993-1996	Berri	Gas lift and Other work	460
	Safaniya	Gas lift	325
	Sadaniya	Tie-in Platforms	300
1994-1997	Berri	WCHF	40
	Khursaniyah	Four Projects	235
	Harmaliyah	Three Projects	110
	Abu Hadriya	Five Projects	195
	Qatif	GOSP-1	55
1995-1998	Qatif	WCHF	40
	Safaniya	GOSP-3	340
	Safaniya	Gas-Lift	250
	Safaniya	Tie-in Platforms	300
	Manifa	Five Projects	1,130
1996-1999	Manifa	Four Projects	1,100
	Suluf	Three Projects	255
1997-2000	Haradh	Four Projects	440
	Khurais	Water Injection	300
1998-2001	Haradh	Four Projects	640
	Qatif	Five Projects	305
	Qatif	Gas-Lift	40
1999-2002	Shaybah	Seven Projects	2,200
2000-2003	Shaybah	Five Projects	760
	Qatif	Five Projects	550

*
N.A. - Not applicable   (1) Gas-Oil Separation plants   (2) Wet Crude Handling Facilities
Source: Compiled from MEED (June) 1990: 23.

Summary of Saudi Arabian Five-Year Development Plan Allocations

Items or Sectors	First Plan 1970-75	% of 1st Plan Total	Second Plan 1975-80	% of 2nd Plan Total	Third Plan 1980-85	% of 3rd Plan Total	Fourth Plan 1985-90	% of 4th Plan Total	Fifth Plan 1990-95	% of 5th Plan Total
Natural resources	—	—	—	—	—	—	—	—	24.5	3.3
Productive Sectors	—	—	—	—	—	—	—	—	45.4	6.0
Economic resources	14,742.	35.7	92,135.0	18.5	261.8	33.5	130.7	13.1	—	—
Human resources	9,258.8	22.4	80,123.9	16.1	129.6	16.6	135.3	13.5	141.1	18.7
Social development	*	*	33,212.8	6.7	61.2	7.8	89.7	9	87.2	11.6
Infrastructure	—	—	112,944.6	22.7	249.1	31.8	144.4	14.4	97.9	13.0
Subtotal	24,000.8	58.2	318,416.3	64.0	701.7	89.7	500.1	50.0	396.1	52.6
Adminstration	7,714.4	18.7	38,1799.2	7.7	31.4	4.0	70.2	7.0	102.1#	13.5
Subsidies and Reserve	—	—	63,478.2	12.7	499.6	6.3	117.3	12.0	—	—
Defense and Security	9,550.0	23.2	78,156.5	15.7	—	—	312.5	31.0	255.1	33.9
Subtotal	17,272.4	41.8	179,813.9	36.0	81.0	10.3	500.0	50.0	357.2	47.4
Total	41,273.2	100	498,230.2	100	782.7	100	1,000.0	100	753.3	100.0

Source: 1) EIU, No. 1, 1990, pp. 1-29
          2) Development Plan, 1970-1975
          3) MEED (May and July) 1975: 8
Note#: a residual figure
Note*: Allocation for this sector is included in Human resources for First Plan

Notes

1. Peter R. Odell, "The Significance of Oil," *The Politics of Middle Eastern Oil*, ed. J. E. Peterson (Washington, D.C.: Middle East Institute, 1983) 5-13. Also see in this collection, Edith Penrose, "International Oil Companies and Governments in the Middle East" 14-31.

2. Another book that discusses changes in world oil markets during the 1930, '40s and '50s is Irvine H. Anderson, *ARAMCO, the United States, and Saudi Arabia: A Study of the Dynamics of Foreign Oil Policy 1933-1950* (Princeton: Princeton U P, 1981). In addition to presenting information that is repeated in several of the sources I have consulted for this lecture, Anderson frankly addresses American "strategies" for exerting influence on the Saudi monarchy for military and commercial reasons. Political commentaries about plans to manipulate Saudi government policy can be found in Dean Achison, *Present at the Creation: My Years at the State Department* (New York: W. W. Norton and Company, 1969), and Leonard Mosley, *Dulles: A Biography of Eleanor, Allen, and John Foster Dulles and Their Family Network* (New York: Dial, 1979).

3. Leonard M. Fanning, *The Shift of World Petroleum Power Away from the United States* (Pittsburgh: Gulf Oil Corporation, 1958) table 4, as cited by Albert Y. Badre and Simon G. Siksek, *Manpower and Oil in Arab Countries* (Beirut: Economic Research Institute, American University of Beirut, 1960) 5.

4. George Lenczowski, *Oil and State in the Middle East* (Ithica: Cornell U P, 1960) 42.

5. Michael Hanifee, "The Impact of Oil on Saudi Arabia," address given at Washington College, Chestertown, MD 1992.

6. Petroleum Press Service as cited by Badre and Siksek, 7-8. For similar verification see Arabian-American Oil Company, *Aramco Handbook: Oil and the Middle East* (Dahran: Aramco, 1968) 78.

7. The tables presented here are compilations of information found in Benjamin Shwaran, *The Middle East, Oil and the Great Powers* (New York: Praeger, 1955) 344-350. It is interesting to note that while the construction of this refinery was indeed expensive, approximately $82 million, it is estimated that the cost to Aramco were recovered from the sale of oil to the U. S. Navy in 1944 and 1945.

8. Richard F. Nyrop, Beryl L. Benderly, Laraine N. Carter, Darrel R. Eglin, and Robert A. Kirchner, *Area Handbook for Saudi Arabia* (Washington: US Government Printing Office, 1974) 265-267.

9. Niel H. Jacobi, *Multinational Oil* (New York: Macmillan Publishing, 1974) 62.

10. Lenczowski 42.

11. Shwadran 363.

12. Aramco, 1968, 148-150.

13. Proposals for pipelines running from the Arabian Gulf to the Mediterranean were not new. Harold Ikes, the US Petroleum Administrator for War, had announced plans for Aramco and the Petroleum Reserves Corporation to build such a pipeline in 1943. The Navy Petroleum Board also entered an agreement with the Petroleum Reserves Aramco Consortium to buy oil pumped through this pipeline. It is not clear how much of the planning came from the Pentagon and how much from the corporations. The plan was never implemented, apparently at the recommendation of the Truman Committee in 1944. For more details see Leonard M. Fanning, *American Oil Operations Abroad* (New York: McGraw-Hill, 1947).

14. Details on the initial planning of these pipelines can be found in Raymond F. Miksell and Hollis B. Chenery, *Arabian Oil: America's Stake in the Middle East* (Chapel Hill: U of North Carolina P, 1949) 55-68.

15. This assertion is verified in several previous citations. Additional tables on the Saudi Arabian Budget Estimates (1948-1958) are found in George A. Lipsky, *Saudi Arabia: Its Peoples, Its Society, Its Culture,* (New Haven: HRAF P, 1959) 317-319. According to the data presented by Lipsky, oil revenues and customs and port receipts (oil duties) financed eighty-six percent of the government's total expenditures in 1953 and 100.3 percent of expenditures in 1958. The ration of oil revenues to expenditures is eighty-eight percent from 1948-1958. These percentages do not change significantly until after Faisal's rule as King.

16. Charles Issawi, *An Economic History of the Middle East and North Africa* (New York: Columbia U P, 1982) 10, 194-211. Lipsky also discusses "domestic trade" in Saudi Arabia during the 1940s and 1950s, see Chapter 17.

17. Naief M. Almtairi, "The Development Process and its Relation to Oil Revenues and Dependence on Imported Labor Market in Saudi Arabia," Pd. D. diss, U Texas at Austin, 1991.

18. Roger Webster, "Bedouins Take the Fruit of Progress," *The Middle East Journal* 91 (May, 1982): 41-58.

19. Mukhtar M. Ballool, "Economic Analysis of the Long-term Planning Investment Strategies for the Oil Surplus Funds in Saudi Arabia: An Optimal Control Approach," diss., U of Houston, 1981.

20. Edmond Y. Asfour, "Prospects and Problems of Economic Development of Saudi Arabia, Kuwait, and the Gulf Principalities," *Economic Development and Population Growth in the Middle East,* eds. Charles A. Cooper and Sidney S. Alexander (New York: American Elsevier Publishing, 1927) 367-398.

21. John Yemma, "Saudis as Producers: A Dream Comes True," *The Christian Science Monitor,* as quoted by Almtairi 123.

22. Ballool 53.

23. Calculated from the tables provided by Lipsky 319-20.

24. Asfour 371 and 379.

25. Badre and Siksek 52.

26. Andrew M. Evans, "The U. S. Corps of Engineers in Saudi Arabia: The Civilian-based Programs," address at Washington College, Chestertown, MD, 1992.

27. John T. Greenwood, "Diplomacy Through Construction: The U.S. Army Corps of Engineers in Saudi Arabia, (Washington, D.C.: Corps of Engineers, 1984) 1.

28. Joan F. Kibler, "Phase Out in Saudi Arabia," *Military Engineer* March-April 1989. Also see Greenwood 2-3; and Victoria Hammond, "Constructing the New World Order: The Case of the U. S. Army Corps of Engineers in Saudi Arabia," paper distributed by the Middle East Studies Association, (Tempe, Middle Eastern Studies Association, 1991) 2.

29. Nasser I. Rashid and Ibrahim Shaheen, *King Fahd and Saudi Arabia's Great Evolution* (Joplin: International Institute of Technology, 1987) 199.

30. Evans; Greenwood 4.

31. Ambassador Twinam, "Address on the Activities of the United States Army Corps of Engineers in Saudi Arabia," Hearing before the Committee on Foreign Affairs, 96th U.S. Congress, House Foreign Affairs Committee, 25 June, 1979. See also, The Saudi Arabian Programs (Winchester, VA: Public Affairs Division of the Middle East Division, Corps of Engineers) 1985.

This point was also discussed by Marc Brewen, "The U. S. Army Corps of Engineers in Saudi Arabia: The Military Programs," address to Washington College, Chestertown, MD, 1992.

32. Ballool 33-35. Figures are quoted at current prices in millions of Saudi Riyals.

33. An important note is that the percentage of exports that were oil-based did not change during this period. The percentage of oil products compared to total exports was 99.7 percent in 1960, 99.7 percent in 1962, 99.2 percent in 1964, and 99.8 percent in 1966. The composition of the oil-based export changed, which consisted of more refined or value-added products. Ibrahim M. Al-Awaji, "Bureaucracy and Society in Saudi Arabia," diss, U of Virginia, 1971, 87.

34. Joy W. Viola, *Human Resource Development in Saudi Arabia: Multinationals and Saudization* (Boston: International Human Resource Development Corporation, 1986) 33.

35. Al-Awaji 147-163. Several outside teams were hired to evaluate the planning needs of the Saudi government, including teams from the Ford Foundation, the United Nations, and the U.S. Federal Reserve. This indicates the level of King Faisal's committment to professional planning.

36. David Edens and William Snavely, *"Planning for Economic Development in Saudi Arabia,"* Middle East Journal (Winter, 1970): 18.

37. Almtairi 113.

38. Listed in order of their entry into the Kingdom.

39. Rodney Wilson, *Banking and Finance in the Arab Middle East* (New York: St. Martin's Press, 1982) 280.

40. Sadig A-H. Malki, "Institutional Inconsistency: A New Perspective on the Role of the State in Development: A Case Study of Saudi Arabia," Ph.D. diss, Washington U, 1991, 47-50.

41. Ramon Knauerhase, *The Saudi Arabian Economy* (New York: Praeger, 1975) 238-239.

42. Jaber A. Al-Shamrani, "The Impact of Economic Development on on the Financial System in Saudi Arabia," MA Thesis, Colorado State U, 1990, 7, 25-31. Al-Shamrani's comments are supported by Rahji El-Mallakh, *Saudi Arabia: Rush to Development* (London: Croom Helm, 1982), and A. N. Young, *The Making of a Fiancial Giant* (New York: New York U P, 1983).

43. Malki 48 and Al-Awaji 143-62.

44. Al-Shamrani 22-25.

45. The early project agreements included Agricultural Bank Management and Training, co-managed by the Saudi Arabian Agricultural Bank and the U.S. Farm Credit Administration; Ministry of Agriculture and Water, co-managed by the Ministry of Agriculture and Water and the U.S. Department of Agriculture; Desalination and Hydroponic, co-managed by the Saudi Arabian Saline Water Conservation Corporation and the U.S. Department of Agriculture; Executive Management Development, organized through cooperative arrangements with U.S. private industry; University Development, designed for King Faisal University with the U. S. Department of Education; Manpower Development and and Vocational Training, co-managed by the Ministry of Labor and the U.S. Department of Labor; and Audit Administration and Training, co-managed by the Saudi Arabian General Control Board and the U.S. Department of Treasury; and Central Procurement and Supply management. These agreements reflected important challenges faced by King Faisal and his planning administrators when they wrote the first and second Five Year Development Plans. At each point in the discussion, the common denominator is the orderly transfer of technology.

46. Saudi Arabian Monetary Agency, Research and Statistics Department, Statistical Summary, 1985, 68-71.

47. The following discussion of the five Five-Year Development Plans will be a compilation of my own research and information taken from Almtairi's, Ballool's, and

Fozan's dissertations. Other references will be directly cited.

48. Central Planning Organization, First Development Plan, 1970-1975, 43.

49. Ministry of Planning, Third Development Plan, 1980-1985, 88.

50. John A. Shaw and David E. Long, *Saudi Arabian Modernization: The Impact of Change on Stability* (New York: Praeger, 1982) 12.

51. John R. Presley, *A Guide to the Saudi Arabian Economy* (New York: St. Martin's, 1984) 12.

52. Third Development Plan, 28, as catagorized by Presley, 1984, 13, and Presley, revised edition, 1990, 12-20.

53. Henry T. Azzam also discusses the transitory stage of development for Saudi Arabia and the other Gulf States in *The Gulf Economies in Transition* (New York: St. Martin's, 1988).

54. Robert Looney, *Economic Development in Saudi Arabia: Consequences of the Oil Price Decline* (Greenwich: JAI, 1990) 88-89.

55. Presley and Westaway 100-101.

56. Mark Heller and Nadav Safran, *The New Middle Class and Regime Stability in Saudi Arabia* (Cambridge, MA: Center for Middle Eastern Studies, Harvard U, 1985).

57. Bandar al-Hajjar and John R. Presley, "Managerial Inefficiencies in Small, Manufacturing Businesses in Saudi Arabia: A Constraint Upon Economic Development," Proceedings of the 1991 British Society for Middle Eastern Studies Conference (London: U of London, 1991). Also see Robert Looney 111-136.

58. Fouad Al-Farsy probably provides the most detailed analysis available of the fourth plan in two books. See *Modernity and Tradition: The Saudi Equation* (London: Kegan Paul International, 1990) 159-164 and *Saudi Arabia: A Case Study in Development* (London: KPI Limited, 1986) 162-177.

59. John R. Presley, "Private Sector Holds Key to Goals of Fourth Plan," *Middle East Economic Digest Special Report: Saudi Arabia* July 1985: 96.

60. Looney 281. There was a sustantial amount of carryover of projects from the third Plan that were completed in the period of the fourth plan. See Looney 36. However, the biggest infrastructure projects had been completed, and the factories at Yanbu and Jubail were quickly coming on line. New projects were not, therefore, of major size in the fourth Plan. For example, the Ministry of Agriculture and Water had by 1988 built 180 dams, only eleven more were planned over the periods of the fourth and fifth Plans. See Almtairi 140.

61. "Saudi Arabia: Revival Predicted in the Early 1990s," *Middle East Economic Digest* 20 Dec. 1986: 60.

62. J. W. Wright, Jr., "Accounting in Saudi Arabia: Imperative Questions for the 1990s," Proceeding of the 1992 British Society for Middle Eastern Studies Conference (St. Andrews: St. Andrews U, 1992), 636-644. The problems of overzelous financing in an economy without a standardized and regulated accounting industry are also addressed in Bandar al-Hajjar, John R. Presley, and J. W. Wright, Jr, "Structural and Attitudinal Impediments to Efficient Capital Distribution in Saudi Arabia's Islamicizing Economy: Implications for Financial Sector Training," Proceedings of the International Seminar on Islamic Economics at the World Bank (Washington, D.C., 1992).

63. R. J. A. Gazzard, "Physical Planning in Saudi Arabia: Aspects of Plan Preparation, Approval and Review," Proceedings of the 1992 British Society for Middle Eastern Studies Conference (St. Andrews: St. Andrews U, 1992) 372-387.

64. John Presley, Tony Westaway, and John Sessions, "Saudi Arabia: Problems of Economic Development in the 1990s," Proceedings of the 1992 British Society for Middle Eastern Studies Conference (St. Andrews: St. Andrews U, 1992) 602-618.

65. Rashid and Shaheen, 188.

66. Almtairi 237.

King Faisal bin Abdulaziz Al-
Saud was mainly responsible for
setting up the Kingdom's intricate
planning structure during the
1960's. His plans set the course for
Saudi Arabia's economic development.

King Khaled bin Abdulaziz Al-
Saud's leadership allowed the
Kingdom to implement the
Second and Third Five-Year
Development Plans. Most of the
Kingdom's infrastructure con-
struction took place during his
reign.

Developing the minds of Saudi Arabia's children has been of primary importance. Education is free to all Saudi citizens.

The Saudi government has built an elaborate university system that allows
all citizens access to higher education. The top picture is of the University
of Petroleum and Minerals in Dhahran. The lower picture is a view of
University Avenue in Riyadh.

Construction expenditures dominated the Saudi budget in the second and third development plans. As a result, new skylines have appeared across the nation. First, a picture reflecting old and new architecture in Riyadh. Second, a picture of Jeddah's skyline in 1991.

Above, a city view of Mecca, the
home of the Grand Mosque.
Right, a general view of the
Riyadh T.V. tower.

Infrastructure construction has rarely been easy, but its results have been spectacular. The King Fahd causeway (top) links Saudi Arabia with Bahrain, while the Taif Roadway allows travelers to pass formerly formidable mountains.

Foreign ventures and direct investment have also played a large part in Saudi Arabia's development. The Pepsi bottling plant in Damman (top) and the tire factory in Jeddah are representative of Saudi-American business ventures.

Water conservation and purification is a major undertaking throughout the Kingdom. However, the efficient use of water has also lead to the beautification of the country. This man-made stream (above) runs through Riyadh's central park. To the left is the water tower in Al-Kharj.

Industrial revenues are still lead by oil-related production. This photograph is of the Arabian Petrochemical Company at Al-Jubail.

The Preservation
of Saudi Traditions

Developing The Archaeology of Saudi Arabia: 15 Years of State Directed Systematic Research

by
Abdullah H. Masry

A vigorous archaeological policy with multifaceted interests has been shaped by the Saudi government, encompassing both short and long term objectives for achievement. This presentation is intended as a brief but comprehensive statement on the contemporary status of, and the developing interest in, archaeology within the Kingdom of Saudi Arabia and those aspects of scholarship and research related to it.

The Government of Saudi Arabia set up a Department of Antiquities in the early 1960s. It was joined then, as it is still, with the Ministry of Education. The government introduced a comprehensive antiquities law which was to provide standard guidelines for the Department's operations and to establish a consultative body, "The High Council for Antiquities." The primary purpose of the Council was to set policies and establish programs consonant with the need for protection, research, and preservation of the country's cultural heritage in accordance with the Antiquities Law.

Over the last two decades Arabian archaeology has undergone a rapid transformation that has affected its relevance and role in the wide context of the study of ancient Near Eastern history. During the late 1960s and early 1970s, the archaeology of Arabia depended on and benefitted from interregional comparisons with the synthesis of archaeological investigations in adjacent regions. This inevitably resulted in a fragmented picture of archaelogical developments. Thus, one tended to see each of the distinct regions within Arabia in relation to the nearest better known cultural areas, Egypt, Iraq, Jordan, Palestine, and Syria, rather than in relation to the rest of the Arabian peninsula.

Although antiquarian interest in the ancient monuments that are located in present day Saudi Arabia is apparent in Arab-Moslem and European travellers' diaries and in the brief reports provided by the much earlier Arab geographers and historians such as al-Hamdani and Yaqut al-Hamawi, the fact remains that Saudi Arabian archaeology is essentially a post mid-twentieth century development. Note must be made of the activities of several European and American antiquarians early in this century: The French Dominican Archaeological Mission of A.J.F. Jaussen and R. Savignac, in the course of three expeditions in 1907, 1909, and 1910, carried out an exhaustive examination of the monuments and inscriptions surviving above ground at the oasis of Tabuk, Madain Saleh, and al-Ula. Mention should also be made of Bernhard

Moritz's visit to al-Qurrayah in the north in 1906 and to Hijaz in 1914. The Czech/American scholar Alois Musil carried out a series of important explorations in the northern Hijaz and the Najd which greatly contributed to knowledge of the ethnography and archaeology of northern Arabia. The explorations of J. Philby (1922), Henry Field, Rychmans, and traditional local historians/antiquarians such as Hamad al-Jassir and Abdulrehman al-Ansari were followed in the 1960s by a string of intermittent expeditions under the auspices of the then newly founded Department of Antiquities and Museums. These included the expeditions of Winnet and Reed (1962 and 1972) and the work of two ex-directors of the American School of Oriental Research in Jerusalem which recorded archaeological and epigraphical sites in the northwestern and northern regions of the Kingdom. Father Albert Jamme of Catholic University, Washington D.C., travelled and worked mostly in Yemen and southern Arabia (1967) and published several articles and books on the ancient inscriptions of Arabia. The British team of Parr, Ryckmans, and Dayton covered the central and northwestern regions in 1968 and 1969. Biddy's book *Looking for Dilmun* (1971) made references to the eastern province of Saudi Arabia, which was specifically dealt with in his earlier publication "Preliminary Survey in East Arabia" (1968). These researchers and their published works demonstrated the increasing need for a controlled and systematic approach to the Kingdom's archaeology.

It was to satisfy this need that the Government-sponsored Comprehensive Archaeological Survey was instigated in 1976. Its aim was to achieve the widest coverage and documentation of the archaeological remains of the entire Kingdom. The program has been active for 14 years and its results are duly reported in *Atlal* an annual publication by the department dedicated to Arabian archaeology.

The Comprehensive Archaeological Survey resulted in the discovery of thousands of sites throughout the Kingdom. Specialized subject surveys were also carried out which included ancient trade routes and Islamic pilgrim caravanserai. Thus the route known as "Darb Zubaydh," the former pilgrim and trade route to and from Mecca, was exhaustively documented over six successive seasons. Each way-station on the route was pinpointed, mapped and recorded. The results of this work are now being used for selective restoration and improvement, including actual reactivation of some of the water reservoirs and basins for the benefit of contemporary populations. The Syrian and Egyptian pilgrim routes along the Red Sea coast and its littoral have also been surveyed, and several early Islamic town-sites have been discovered.

Three successive seasons were devoted to the investigation of ancient mining sites in Arabia. Specialists from the Colorado School of Mines working alongside local Saudi archaeological staff were involved in the investigation and documentation of forts. The three expeditions worked within three fairly restricted areas within the Arabian shield, northwest Hijaz, and areas in the southwestern region, and located over 200 ancient gold, silver, and copper mines as well as semi-precious stone quarries. Another specialized survey focussing on rock art and epigraphy was initiated in 1985 and produced in the last six seasons the documentation for over 1000 rock art and epigraphic sites in the northern and southern parts of the country.

It should be noted that the comprehensive specialized archaeological survey projects were planned from the outset as the pilot of future systematic large scale excavations. Limited test excavations were carried out as a part of group survey work and several sites of prehistoric importance were excavated on a "rescue operation." In addition, large scale archaeological excavations were part of the permanent field training program of King Saud University in Riyadh. The discovery of the final first-millennium B.C. city of al-Faw is the prime example of that effort; another is the early Islamic town-site of ar-Rabbatha near the holy city of Medina.

Apart from these excavations, large scale excavations of several potentially important sites were started in 1985, including Madain Saleh and Taima in northwest Saudi Arabia, the Shahran tomb fields in the eastern province, and the third millennium B.C. neolithic site of Thummamah in the central province. The second first-millennium B.C. sites of Sihi and Ukhdud in the southern region were also part of the initial efforts. Fifth and third millennium B.C. sites of al-Ubaid in the eastern province provide evidence of the earliest littoral settlement in the coast areas of Saudi Arabia. Excavations at early paleolithic sites such as Dawadmi in the central province and Shuhaythia in the north brought the dating of early man's settlement in the Arabian Peninsula to one million years ago.

Thus, from our present understanding of the archaeology of Saudi Arabia, based on the results of surveys and initial excavation, we can postulate a general framework for the cultural and chronological sequences from the period of early man's manifestations to the well-developed prehistoric cultures which preceded literary and early agricultural settlements and which, by comparison with other sites of the ancient Near East, suggest a dating of circa sixth and fifth-millennium B.C. The early neolithic phase in Arabia is abundantly represented by the vast number of sites that are found on the borders of the great Arabian deserts, the Rub al-Khali, the Nafud, and Dhana. They clearly suggest environmental and climate condition difficult from today's extremely dry and hot conditions.

During the critical epochs of the third and second millennia B.C., as measured by the standard chronology of Near Eastern archaeology, Arabia saw the emergence of the peculiar settled/nomadic interplay. An enduring characteristic of the peninsula, it has puzzled and intrigued historical interpretation from that of the 14th century A.D. Arab social historian and philosopher Ibn Khaldun to those of contemporary analysts. In the late second and into the first millennium B.C., we find the existence of well developed urban centres throughout greater Arabia exhibiting fully developed literary, religious and political structures. Several thousand early Arabic inscriptions, such as Thamudic, Musnad al-Uanubi, Nabatean, etc., have been located during the epigraphic survey. Recent investigation by rock art specialists and epigraphers have discovered new evidence regarding the possibility of the independent evolution and development of a writing system within the Arabian Peninsula. Evidence suggests that the alphabets of one of the oldest writings of Arabia, known as Thamudic, evolved from a long process of schematisation and simplification of human and animal figures. With the start of the Islamic period, the archaeological record begin to witness a cultural vitality, one which would assert itself over a vast area.

With regard to time-space interpretations, the chronology of Saudi Arabia's archaeology clearly reveals the continuous presence of man in the peninsula from the earliest paleotithic to the present age. About 100 Acheulean, 195 Mousterean, 197 Neolithic and 166 Chalcolithic sites are recorded from different parts of the country. The monuments of the Islamic period stand out more clearly than those of the earlier periods for obvious reasons: they are better preserved, are representation of an early modern culture, and they are historically and abuntantly documented. Nevertheless, archaeological reconnaissance at these sites has modified the picture by showing that the significance of the Arabian heartland was greater than has sometimes been realized. The surviving archaeological record and the continuing explorations of Arabian archaeology afford ample data, which illustrates the peninsula's wide and divergent networks of cultural relations dating from prehistoric and early historic times.

Extensive conservation and restoration of historic buildings has been part of the Department of Antiquities' series of projects. The old capital of Najd, Dar'iyya, which is located about 20km north of Riyadh, the King Abdulaziz palace and Qasr Masmak in Riyadh, the Mosque of Ibrahim in Al-Hasa, Eastern Province, Bait Nasif in Jeddah and numerous other watch towers, castles, forts and mosques throughout the Kingdom have been restored and preserved by the department during the last 15 years. The Government of Saudi Arabia has allocated large amounts of money for the restoration and preservation of old buildings in the Kingdom. During the five-year plan for 1985-1990, an estimated 180 million Saudi riyals were allocated for the restoration and conservation of old buildings, castles, and other monuments in the Kingdom.

The rapid development and expansion of towns and cities in the Kingdom has created increased potential that archaeological sites will be disturbed. To protect them, the department has prepared a program to enclose with fences those archaeological sites which are located near towns or cities. During the current five-year plan, over 46 million Saudi riyals were spent to protect 185 sites with 195,000 meters of fencing.

Museums have been constructed in several large cities of the Kingdom. A national archaeological and ethnographical museum with an estimated cost of about one billion Saudi riyals is under construction in the capital city of Riyadh. A network of local museums, located at Taima, al-Ula, Domat al-Jundal, Hofuf, Wadi Dawasir, Majran, Jizan, and Qasim also have been built, at a total cost of about 200 million Saudi riyals. Each local museum reflects the particular archaeological and historical identities of its specific area and controls all archaeological activities such as surveys, excavations, preservation, and restoration projects for the area. Regional museums at Damman, Jeddah, and other major cities are planned, as well as two Islamic museums to be installed in the Holy Cities of Mecca and Medina. Their estimated cost is about 500 million riyals. The Department of Antiquities has a well developed publications section, which publishes and supports publications on the archaeology and history of Arabia. *Atlal, The Journal of Saudi Arabian Archaeology,* is published annually and includes reports of on-going research and excavations in the Kingdom. In addition, provision has been made for specialized monographs and publications on specific subjects as well as for posters depicting the antiquities of the Kingdom. Several other types of publications are also planned.

All the excavations, research and restoration programs, and publications are sponsored entirely by the Government of Saudi Arabia. Compared with expenditures by many countries in the world, the amount the Saudi government has spent on antiquity preservation during the last 15 years are unparrelled. One billion Saudi riyals were allocated for archaeological activities during the years of 1965-70, and, as cited earlier, the National Museum in Riyadh will cost more than a billion Saudi riyals.

The advances in Arabian archaeology show that increased understanding of cultural interrelations can be anticipated as new information is uncovered. It is clear that Arabia has occupied a central position with regard to many cultures in adjacent lands at various times in its history.

The foregoing account is, inevitably, a very generalized and sketchy outline of a few of the projects which have been sponsored and undertaken by the Directorate General of Archaeology and Museums in the last few years. Without doubt, the success of these efforts is due chiefly to the generous support that archaeological research receives from His Majesty's Government.

Throughout the previous five-year plans as well as the present one, financial allocations for archaeological activities enabled the Directorate to launch and continue programs of research, restoration, preservation of monuments, and the establishment of museum networks and other related archaeological activities. In addition, this support makes it was possible to secure the participation of prominent archaeologists and institutions from different parts of the world. Some of these include Harvard University, Southwestern University, University of Texas, University of Missouri , and the University of California, the Institute of Archaeology in the United Kingdom, as well as CNRS in Paris. These institutions are just a few among those who have actively participated in our survey and research programs over the past 15 years.

In my lecture at the Smithsonian Institution, I presented seventy-seven slides of archaeological sites located throughout the Kingdom. It was impossible to print all of those pictures in this collection, but I have provided selected sets of photographs for readers' use. I hope they help you realize the magnificence of Saudi Arabia's archaelogical sites.

Entrance to a tomb at Madain Saleh.

Various stone carvings: (top right) Stone pillars near Al-Rajajeel; (left) carved stone block with an animal relief from the seventh century, B.C.; (bottom right) pteroglyph on a stone face at Najran.

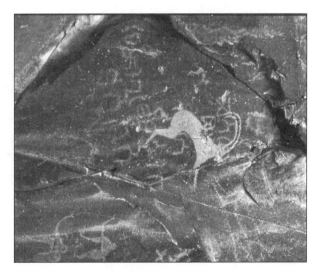

Scenes from Madain Saleh.

Buildings from antiquity: (top) The site at Qurayat al-Fau; (above left) another scene from Qurayat al-Fau; (above right) the ancient al-Rass tower.

(above) Ruins at al-Jouf; (left) the Omar ibn Khafib mosque in al-Jouf.

Buildings from Khamis Mushayt.

Spinning the Tale of Truth:
Oral Traditions in Arab Culture

by
Saad Abdullah Sowayan

Since the medieval period, Arabic traditions of narrative tales and oral poetry have been the literary genres that are represented throughout the Middle East and North Africa.[1] In Saudi Arabia, Arabic's oral traditions are preserved in the form of Nabati poetry, a vernacular poetry which was popular among the bedouin tribes living in the Arabian peninsula. The indigenous home of Nabati poetry is Nadj, the vast territory that surrounds the central Arabian plateau, and the diction of this poetry conforms to the colloquial speech of that region. In this paper I will discuss the role Nabati poetry has played in Saudi Arabia's literary tradition, and then I will talk about the Saudi peoples' attempts to preserve this tradition through the organization of culture festivals and poetry competitions in the Kingdom. Of particular note is the festival at Al-Jenadriyah.

The word *nabati* originally refers to the language of the Nabataeans. However, after centuries of transitions, its meaning was eventually extended by the early Arab philologists until it came to be applied loosely to any speech which did not strictly conform to the rules of classical Arabic. It is in this latter sense that the word was applied by compilers to the vernacular poetry of Arabia, in order to set it apart from the well-established and highly respected classical tradition. Thus, this usage of the word *nabati* is not intended to imply that this poetry is linked in any way to the Nabataeens, but means only that it is composed in Arabian peninsula vernacular rather than in classical, literary Arabic.

Nabati poets rarely use the term *nabati* in reference to themselves or to their poetry, and many of them do not even know this sense of the word.[2] It is not certain when or by whom the term was first used in this context. The first recorded use of the word *nabati* is in a poem by Abu Hamzih al-Amrim a nabati poet who died over four centuries ago. W. G. Palgrave, who claims to have traversed Arabia in 1962, mentions nabati poetry three times in his diaries.[3] R. F. Burton also mentions nabati poetry, but mistakes nabati for Nabataean.[4] The term now appears in the titles of many printed collections and anthologies.[5]

The nabati poet may be a town amir, a tribal sheikh, a desert warrior, a daring marauder, a poor farmer, or a member of the urban elite. As in ancient times, the people of pre-modern Arabia were a nation of poets. Poetic composition was not merely an artistic vocation practiced by professionals exercising their skills in composing panegyrics to wealthy patrons or in entertaining spectators and passive audiences. Rather, poetic letters and rituals played an important role in the Arab social order, preserving both tribal history and also providing an intermixture of poetic recitation with narrative prose.[6] Tribal chiefs and town amirs as well as relatives and friends communicated with each other through poems. Territories, grazing areas, waterholes, desert roads and stations, grievances, threats, battles, and other events, were all were recorded and described in poems. Thus, as Ignaz Goldziher observes about the pre-Islamic Arab oral poetic tradition,[7] Nabati poetry deals with a variety of topics ranging from the sublime to the most mundane and pertaining to collective as well as personal issues, including bedouin life's adventures, its comic moments, its feuds, its hardships, its hospitality, and its warfare.

Nabati poetry is the product of a heroic age characterized by political turmoil and inter-tribal feuds. The incessant raids and forays of the desert Arabs of pre-modern Arabia were celebrated in poems composed and red by tribal poets and heroes. Major battles were generally preceded by a period of mobilization during which poems were exchanged by opponents. Such wars of words were part of the sportive attitude generally held by desert Arab's toward fighting. On the way to a battle, poets composed verses to challenge the enemy and instill courage in their own party. The circumstances of their fight and the warriors' acts of gallantry were recorded in verse. Similarly, poems were composed to mourn fallen heroes and to criticize those who had fled in battle. Sometimes, the strength and worthiness of the enemy were praised if they had fought bravely and gallantly.

The most stirring of the Nabati poems are the compositions of nomadic chiefs and desert knights who employed their poetic skills not to amuse or entertain, but to press for a course of action, to reveal a plan, to declare war, to deliver a threat, to challenge a foe, to sue for peace, to appeal for assistance, to celebrate a victory, to document an honorable deed, or to boast about a chivalrous act. Their verses are registers of their adventures and the roles they played in shaping the events of their time. In addition to chiefs and knights, each tribe had a host of poets. As the militia unsheathed their swords, the poets unleashed their tongues with verses that flew like sharp arrows that symbolically conquered enemy tribes. In big assemblies, the tribe's poet was expected to be alert, quick-witted, and able to cogently and eloquently argue the case of the tribe. He kept in his head any blood debt owed to his tribe by others, and he constantly urged his tribesman to redress the balance and cleanse their honor. The appeal of their poetry lies in the fact that it faithfully depicts in a rich language a nomadic existence that is heroic, chivalrous, and free.

An important part of the Nabati tradition revolves around the emotional presentation of the poems written. Singing and loud vocalization are not only signs of sincerity and rhetoric, they also help the poet measure the rhythm of his verses. For Nabati poets, meter translates into rhyme, and scansion into singing or chanting. The Nabati poet views his meters musically, and determines whether or not his scansion is correct by singing them. The relation of singing to composition is indicated by the expression *y' addil lhun* which refers to the act of composition and which means "to harmonize some tunes" or "to straighten some rhythm." A poet may call his composition *mahkam al-fann*, meaning that its verses are of a perfectly measured rhythm. Sometimes the rhythms of the poem is guided by loud pounding which beats rhythmically against the poet's rib-cage.

The distinction between oral and written modes of composition and transmission are blurred in Nabati poetry because the goal of the writer is to build a poem for recitation. Whether literate of illiterate, a Nabati poet will polish a poem many times before presenting it to the public. And, with regard to transmission, the possible illiteracy of the poet does not rule out the record of his work in writing. It was not uncommon for an illiterate poet to open his poem by imploring a scribe to take his verses down on paper. By the same token, a poet's literacy did not preclude the possibility that the poet would make an oral presentation only. However, a literate Nabati poet would usually collect his poems in a *diwan* which he would inscribe in his own hand. Often, wealthy illiterates had their scribes write down their poems and the poems that had been composed in their honor. These collections were sent to distant relatives, patrons, or friends.

Whether written or not, it is pertinent to stress once more the important social function and the serious attitude with which Nabati poetry was and is viewed by a native audience. Just as the form and content of Nabati poetry are governed by culturally circumscribed aesthetic conventions, the poetry itself exercises unrivalled influence on the culture and society of Arabia; this is especially true in the pre-modern times in the Nadj region. People of the time are said to have quoted Nabati verses and compose them on all occasions, and they listened to poetry not merely to be entertained but, more importantly, to be edified and uplifted. Poetry was said to provide the best guide for discerning men, since it provided them with a system of values and models for ideal conduct. Poetry was also called the "driving stick" of men, because it spurred them to act with manliness in defense of tribal honor and with communal interests in their hearts.

Recitations of poetry also had and have a distinct political dimension. On the whole, and especially among the nomads, poetry was viewed as a vehicle for social and political change before being a source of amusement, and its composition and transmission were a public obligation and responsibility. In the desert, every tribesman considers it his duty to memorize and propagate verses that glorify his tribe and recount the deeds of its heroes. Of course, there are active and passive bearers of poetry; but the poetic tradition is considered a public register and a public trust for traditions that each generation passes on to the next. It contains historical and genealogical information recorded in rich poetic language that gives a meaning and permanence and makes its recitation an emotionally charged experience which is eagerly anticipated.

In the early part of this century, the popularity of Nabati poetry continued. There was no special time or setting required for reciting Nabati poetry. Whenever people, usually men, gathered together, they would often engage in short contests for poetry recitation. During these contests, silence reigned over the assembly and strict attention was paid to the message in the poem. Wilfred Thesinger, who lived for some years time with the desert Arabs, wrote that "they (bedouin men) find it an almost unendurable hardship to keep silent. Yet that evening when someone started to recite poetry, a hush fell over the camp, [...] One after the other they gathered round, silent except when they repeated the final line of each verse."[8] To interfere with the poet or to interrupt his recitation is a serious offense. Even the slightest sign of disinterest by members of a poet's audience was considered to be a great insult.[9]

Generally speaking, especially as the Nabati tradition approached modern dates, poetic recitation alternates with prose narration with the lives of various poets and the events celebrated in their lives. The wording in the poetry is fixed, but the prose narrative is discursive and loosely structured. The narrative that is associated with a particular poem is called its *salfih* (pl. sawalif). The telling of *sawalif* and the recitation of poetry are termed the discourse of real men (*kalam ar-rajal*), since only discerning men can grasp their deeper significance. Although their are accomplished poetesses, poetry is mainly a male domain, but women and children are more often passive but eager and attentive members of the audience when allowed to attend.

The most favored time for telling *sawalif* and reciting poetry is at night, when men gather around the hearth in the tent of a gallant nomad or in the coffee-chamber of a noble citizen. There is often a ritual nature to these events. Behind the hearth sets the host, who is responsible for providing hospitality to his guests. He is usually assisted by another person in the preparation of coffee and in the maintenance of the fire, and a young man, usually the son of the host, is always standing up with a coffee pot in his left hand and small china cups is his right, pouring coffee for the assembly of guests. The poet or guest of honor sits at the right hand of the host. In a nomadic tent this assembly of men is separated from women by a thin curtain. The guest poet will recite a poem and offer the *sawalif* that occasioned its composition. At his conclusion, other men may respond with a poem of their own, or, if the historical representations in the guest's poem differs from that of another well established poem, then one of the members of the audience may recite the more famous poem. From there, the discussion may drift to which tribe has the best poets, or who is the poet most esteemed by the people and whose verses are the most appealing. Such questions can split the assembly into different sides and lively discussions will erupt interspersed with choice poetic examples. At this stage, emotional presentation and rhetoric play an important part in the performance context of the evening.

Up until the 1960s, people composed and recited poetry in this sort of ritual function all year round, but in the summer there was always an extraordinary flurry of poetic activity. In the rainy season, the farmers were busy plowing and sowing their fields, while the nomads would disperse into the desert. Summer, on the other hand, was the time of reunion when the various lineages congregated at their tribal walls and when the nomads and settlers came together to renew their social and economic relationships. Communication between these groups became intense, and visitation very frequent. The poets of the settled areas and the bedouin poets would organize forums for the exchange of their poetry. For these men, the composition and recitation of poetry and the spinning of narratives were ways to review and synthesize the events of the past and to conceive future plans. At the end of the summer, the poets lamented the departure of the nomadic tribes and the separation of friends and lovers.

It is unfortunately true that the performance context of Nabati poetry is disappearing rapidly. The economic and political changes in Arabia have severely curtailed the social role of Nabati poetry and constrained its function. Interest in Nabati poetry is on the wane, and radio and television, along with phonographic and tape recording machines, which have reached even the bedouin tents in the desert, have usurped or radically altered the traditional public roles of composers and reciters of Nabati poetry. Furthermore, the number of active bearers of the tradition was becoming continually smaller.

I put the last sentence in the past tense because there is a growing community of people in the Kingdom who are intent on using modern technological advancements to properly preserve the traditions that surround Nabati poetry. Special programs on Nabati poetry are broadcast on a weekly basis from the radio and television stations in Saudi Arabia, Kuwait, and Qatar. The programs are very popular among certain segments of the population, and there is usually a close rapport between the program and its viewers. Listeners frequently write the host of the program requesting to hear a certain poet or a specific poem. The hosts of these programs are authorities on Nabati poetry with wide connections with the currently popular Nabati poets. Some are accomplished poets in their own right. In order to keep the ritual tradition alive, the readings are done on sets with large tents furnished with pillows and a fireplace with all the necessary utensils for making coffee. The program is interspersed with the showing of various scenes from desert and bedouin life.

A more ambitious under taking is the Kingdom's grand folk festival at Al-Jenadriyah, sponsored by The University of Riyadh, which aims to remind the people of Saudi Arabia of their cultural heritage. Although the festival has grown to include a full fair, camel and horse races, dancing competitions, and craft and book expeditions, the central part of the festival is a series of Nabati poetry contests. The festival's main contests, and a variety of other events, are recorded and preserved in the University's archives.

Ten years ago Riyadh's King Saud University devised an annual festival devoted to vernacular poetry. Some members of the faculty of Folklore and Dialectics did have an academic interest in organizing the festival, but the festival was part of a much larger move by the University to provide outreach programs to the community. Feeling the strain of hectic socio-economic change, many Saudi citizens were eager to find a glimpse of their peoples' pre-modern traditions. After two years operating just as a poetry festival, it was decided to combine the poetry festival with the King's very successful camel races, also traditionally held at Al-Jenadriyah, and the idea of organizing a grand folk festival emerged. The cause was greatly assisted by the enthusiasm and support of H.R.H. Crown Prince Abdullah bin Abdulaziz, who is always keen on fostering peoples' pride in local traditions and Saudi-specific cultural identity.

Many government officials joined in the effort to make the expanded al-Jenadriyah festival a success. A preliminary committee headed by HRH Prince Bdar bin Abdulaziz, Vice-Chairman of the National Guard, and including H.R.H. Prince Faisal bin Fahd, Head of the General Presidency of Youth Welfare, was set up to draft a plan for the new festival. Based on their plan, the first Annual Festival for Culture and Heritage opened at Al-Jenadriyah in 1985, with the goals of acquainting the Kingdom's younger generation with the heritage of their grandparents.

The festival, that has come to be known simply as Al-Jenadriyah, now includes programs and shows sent by the governors and mayors of every region and town in Saudi Arabia. In addition, it includes a fair with representations of traditional activities by artists, craftsmen, folk troupes, and poets. Other displays include a traditional farm, with well water drawn by camel power; a traditional *suq* or marketplace, with over seventy shops selling traditional crafts, masonry work, metal smith goods and weaving products; exhibitions of archaeological finds; a book display yielding over fifteen hundred titles; a highly successful art exhibition, that includes a children's art display; shows by the trainers of camels, falcons, and horses; booths serving traditional Arab cuisine; and the presentation of plays and lectures on a wide range of subjects. The first day of the festival opens with two camel races, attended each year by King Fahd. Prizes for the first two hundred winners (over two thousand riders enter the race annually) exceeds 2,500,000 SR. Following the presentation of the grand purse, there is a colorful pageant staged by the four hundred groups that participate in the festival.

Recitations of poetry begin at 10:30 each evening, with many of the Arab world's most famous poets attending. Each year an average of eighty poets present their verses to festival guests. One of the most popular parts of these events are the poetic duals, some of which are planned and others that develop spontaneously as the nights progress. Selections from these performances are broadcast by Saudi radio and television, and many of the poems are collected and published in annual editions based on the festival's proceedings.

In addition to providing a forum for exposing the Kingdom's youth to their heritage, Al-Jenadriyah has helped to strengthen political unity in the Kingdom by fostering cultural unity. It is not just the only event were representatives from all regions of the country come together for a shared cultural experience, it is a place were tradition and transition come together. It is the new technology that makes the event possible, and it is modern equipment that allows for the presentation of traditional culture to masses of people. The festival also allows the Kingdom's ancient artistic traditions to mix with new developments in the arts; the relatively new Saudi national symphony performs at the festival too. And, the new book exhibit is the biggest market for the sale of books on Saudi folklore, society and tradition. The Al-Jenadriyah festival also helps dispel misconceptions by many that ours is a drab country populated only by puritanical zealots.

As Al-Jenadriyah demonstrates, Saudi Arabia is a country with a long history, an intricate social structure, and rich traditions of great complexity, depth and diversity. At the same time, the commitment that the government has made to the funding and organization of the Al-Jenadriyah festival illustrates its sincere interest in preserving true Saudi traditions.

The following photographs will give readers a taste of the activities at the Al-Jenadriyah festival. They will help you understand the diversity and strength of Saudi Arabia's cultural traditions.

Notes

1. For recent publications with more extensive discussions of Arabic's narrative traditions see: Suzanne Pinckney Stetkevych, *Reorientations: Studies in Arabic and Persian Poetry*, ed., (Bloomington: Indiana University Press, forthcoming, 1993) and *Abu Tammam and the Poetics of the Abbasid Age*, (Leiden: E. J. Brill Publishers, 1991); J. W. Wright, Jr., "Women: Islam's Willing Martyrs, *Dying for Love: The Discourse of the Female Martyr*, Evan Blythen, ed., (Albany: SUNY Press, forthcoming, 1993); David Penault, *Story-telling Techniques in the Thousand and One Nights*, (Leiden: E. J. Brill, 1992); Fedwa Malti-Douglas, *Woman's Word: Gender and Discourse in Arabo-Islamic Writing*, (Princeton: Princeton University Press, 1991); and Sandra Naddaff, *Arabesque: Narrative Structure and the Aesthetics of Repetition in 1001 Nights*, (Evanston: Northwestern University Press, 1991).

2. A Nabati poet is called by his peers simply a poet (sa' ir or gassad), and his work is called poetry (*si' ir* or *gisad*). The poet usually introduces his composition as gisidih "ode," *abyat* "verses," *gaf* or *gifan* "rhymes," *gol* or *gil* "contemplated utterances," *kalam* "solemn address," *amtal* or *mitayil* "allegories," or *jawab* "responses."

3. W. G. Palgrave, *Narrative of a Year's Journey through Central and Eastern Arabia*, vol I, (London: Macmillan and Co., 1865), 169, 281, 335.

4. Richard Burton, *Personal Narratives of a Pilgramme to al-Madinah and Meccah*, (New York: Dover Publications Inc, 1984), 224.

5. E.g. Kh. M. al-Faraj, *Diwan al-Nanbat* , 2 vols (Damascus: Matba'at al-Taraqqi, 1952); F. al-Rashid, *Shu' ara al-Rass al-Nabatiyun*, 2 vols (Damascus: al-Matba'ah al-Hashimiyah, 1965); A. Kh. al-Hatam, *Khiyar ma Yaltaqat min al-Shi'r al-Nabat*, (Damascus: al-Matba'ah al-'Umamiyah, 1968); M. S. ibn Sayhan, *al-Tuhfah al-Rashidiyah fi al-Ash'ar al-Nabatiyah*, 2 vols (Kuwait: Matba'at at al-Risalah, 1965 and 1969); A. Babutayn, *al-Majmu'ah al-bahiyah min al-ash'ar al-nabtiyah* (Riyadh: Maktabat al-Riyad al-Hadithah, 1969); S. H. ibn Huraywil, *Diwan al-Nabat al-Hadith* (Beirut: Matabi' al-Wafa', 1374 A.H.); A.I. al-Hadhdhal, *Mukhtarat min al-Shi'r al-Nabati al-Mu'asir*, (Riyadh: Matabi' al-Shihri, 1392 A.H.).

6. The content and function of poetry in the Arabian desert can be compared to Somali nomadic poetry, of which B. W. Andrzejewski writes in "The Poetry in Somali Society," New Society, no. 25, (21 March, 1963): 22-24; and *Somali Poetry: An Introduction*, (Oxford: The Clarendon Press, 1964).

7. Ignaz Goldziher, *A Short History of Classical Arabian Literature*, J. de Somogyi, trans. (Hildeshein: Georg Olms Verslagsbuchhandlung, 1966), 12.

8. Wilfred Thesinger, *Arabian Sands*, (New York: E. P. Dutton and Company, 1959), 72.

9. Charles Dougherty, *Travels in Arabia Deserta*, 2 vols., (New York: Randon House, 1921) 306; and A. Ibn Khamis, *al-Adab al-sha'bi fi Jazirat al-'Arab*, (Beirut: Dar al-Kitab al-Lubnani, 1958) 13.

At the Al-Jenadria
festival: Camels, camels
everywhere.

A metalsmith (above) and a potter display their respective arts at the Al-Jenadriyah festival.

A weaver demonstrates his skills at the Al-Jenadria festival.

The Islamic Fundamentalism of the Wahhabi Movement

by
Jaafar S. Idris

The term "fundamentalist" is most often used to describe a twentieth century Protestant movement in the United States that was "in opposition to modernist tendencies in American religious and secular life."[1] The basis of this movement is found in nineteenth century millennial beliefs that in 1909 were published in the United States as *The Fundamentals.*[2] But while this term describing organized efforts against the complete secularization of states originated in America, fundamentalist activities calling for a return to religiously- and morally-oriented governance seem to be a world-wide phenomenon; certainly it is seen in Buddist, Christian, Hindu, Jewish, Muslim, and Zoroastrian communities around the globe. There are, it would seem, among adherents of all religions groups, people who have decided to return to beliefs based on literal interpretations of the religious texts they believe divine.

The most well-known form of fundamentalism, at least the most repeatedly maligned by Western journalists, politicians, and scholars, however, is Islamic fundamentalism. Not all people in these professions paint a negative picture of the Muslim community, but too many do. The most common and gross mistake made in American print are the assertions that Islamic fundamentalism is a homogeneous movement that can be defined, or that a particular ethnic group can be identified and attacked as Moslem fundamentalists. These assertions are, of course, far from true. Islam, like Buddhism, Christianity, Hinduism, Judaism, and Zoroastrianism, has seen the development of various factions within the religion. On a broad scale, the Shi'a and Sunni movements form the most distinctive sects of the Moslem religion, but within these sects are widely disparate groups and movements. Unfortunately, all are dubbed by Western media as fundamentalist.

Why is it that the Western media as well as public figures use one term to describe such a diverse religious population? What is it that justifies the use of a simple phrase to describe Muslim groups, organizations, and even entire states? The answer cannot simply be that Muslim fundamentalists reject secularism because this position is no doubt shared by other non-Islamic but religiously-oriented, anti-secular groups. Somehow, Muslim fundamentalism has become confused with anti-Westernism or anti-Americanism.

Because of this, members of the Muslim world are often presented in American reports and stories as threats to Western civilization. It is paradoxical that this accusation is often made by Western moral or religious leaders who are themselves proponents of using "moral majorities" to influence government policies in their own countries. Certainly, the equation of "Western" with "secular" misrepresents the real political situation in Canada, Europe and the United States. By the same token, characterizing all Muslims as anti-Western is equally misrepresentative, as is dubbing any individual Muslim who expresses a non-Western opinion as fundamentalist. Worse still, the Western press has associated Islamic fundamentalism with terrorism, acts of violence that make a genuine Muslim shudder, both as a human being and as a believing Muslim for the Prophet of Islam condemns the killing of non-combatants.

Misconceptions abound, including the implementation of democracy. On the one hand, people would applaud democratic ideals. This is especially true for Muslims because much in democratic practice parallels Islamic notions of governance. On the other hand, it is surely chauvinistic to assume that all democratic institutions and values must be identical to those found in twentieth century North America or Europe. The wish to develop an indigenous style of democracy does not necessarily represent an anti-Western agenda, although it has been portrayed as such by the media.

All this is not to deny the fact that there is a phenomenon in the Muslim world which can be described as fundamentalist. The question is about how to characterize that phenomenon. What, then, is Islamic fundamentalism? Formulating an answer first requires examining the Western-Christian perspective. The Christian fundamentalist movement is characterized by the belief that the Bible is the divine word of God, and that a literalist interpretation of the virgin birth of Jesus, Jesus's second coming, the promise of eternal life in heaven, as well as eternal punishment in hell for sinners, is the correct Biblical interpretatism. Moreover, the Christian fundamentalist movement feels it necessary for believers to pursue evangelical activities.

If judged by these criteria for Christian fundamentalism, all Muslims appear to be fundamentalists. Islamic fundamentalists, also believe that Jesus was born of a Virgin, that he will return to earth on Judgement Day, and that an eternal heaven and eternal hell are necessary to a monotheist cosmology. And, like Christians who believe in the Bible, Wahhabi Muslims believe that the Qur'an, as the infallible word of God, should be interpreted literally. Muslims are also asked to spread the word of God to as many people as possible.

In what sense, then, can fundamentalism be a special characteristic of some Muslim individuals, groups, or movements? The distinguishing characteristic appears to lie in the sense of urgency some feel about advocating the fundamentals of Islam. People who experience this sense of urgency genuinely find justifications for their ideals in the literal understanding of Islamic texts, and they believe that other Muslims neglect, are ignorant of, or are not committed to Islamic fundamentals. Such fundamentalists argue that their philosophy is broad enough to embrace people of any age or profession but that it must react against external cultural intervention. Judged from this perspective on Islamic fundamentalism, Abd al-Wahhab, the religious founder of Saudi Arabia, was a paragon among Muslim fundamentalist leaders.

Abd al-Wahhab spent most of his long life, 1703 to 1792, studying the Islamic fundamentals and the methods of obtaining religious knowledge, while urging the necessity of establishing a Muslim state to propagate and defend the faith. He devoted his life to teaching and advocating Islamic fundamentals, criticizing those who rejected them. His interpretation of the sacred texts was literal, and he frequently used the word "fundamental" in many of his influential tracts, leaving no doubt as to his moral and philosophical position, one that drew many followers.

Today's fundamentalism, whether Islamic or non-Islamic, is characterized by its rejection of Western secularism. Abd al-Wahhab was not concerned with other parts of the world, and certainly the notion of Western secularism was beyond his comprehension. His was a local movement. Nevertheless, he faced a secularism of another brand, called *jahiliya* (ignorance), the Islamic term for any system of social life based on human ideas and whims rather than on divine guidance. Abd al-Wahhab insisted that the governance of tribal chiefs was *jahiliya* if they did not implement Islamic law, if they, for example, deprived females of their legitimate inheritances or if they refused to exercise Islamic law on an equal and just basis.

Undoubtedly Abd al-Wahhab was able to awaken people to the evils of *jahiliya* because he possessed an essential hallmark of a good teacher: he paid attention to his audience and addressed them in the most appropriate manner. Ali, the fourth Caliph, is reported to have said, "Speak to people in a way they can understand. Do you want them to disbelieve God and His Prophet?"[3] Abd al-Wahhab heeded that advice. Whenever he wrote to scholars outside his bedouin community, he appropriately used classical Arabic, but when he addressed his own people, he used colloquial words and expressions. With the exception of his personal letters, his style was legalistic, concise, and somewhat terse; he wasn't given to flights of rhetoric.

In contrast to Ibn Taymiya, who resorted to elaborate rational arguments to buttress and defend Qur'anic teachings on theological matters, Abd al-Wahhab was content to use simple religious textual evidence and sought to avoid the subject of philosophical-theology altogether. Whereas Ibn Taymiya lived in Damascus at a time when it teemed with philosophers, theologians, Sufis, scholars, and scientists, Abd al-Wahhab lived in a simple cultural milieu requiring no erudition. Yet Abd al-Wahhab knew full-well that when advocates of social reform express new ideas, they are likely to encounter challenge, criticism, and opposition. Consequently, he was careful to equip his followers with simple arguments that could be employed to defend their beliefs when members of opposition groups tried to embarrass or defy them.

Abd al-Wahhab was aware that he was not only a preacher and a scholar, but also the leader of a movement seeking to effect real change in society. He believed that the dissemination of knowledge was a first step and a necessary condition for effecting change, but he realized that this alone would not be enough. He was convinced of the need for power to realize his goals, so he sought the support of tribal chiefs and Arab heads of state. One of these chiefs was Mohammed bin Saud, the ruler of Dar'iyya, who accepted Abd al-Wabbah's teachings and agreed to defend the movement. Thus started one of the strongest Islamic militant movements which did not shrink from engaging in war with its opponents. The relationship of Abd al-Wahhab and Mohammed bin Saud laid the foundation for the government that would lead to the unification of the Kingdom of Saudi Arabia.

Many movements, Islamic or non-Islamic, are short-lived because the tenets or beliefs do not have a strong enough hold on the minds of followers. Thus, once the followers face adverse circumstances or situations different from those that induced them to join the group in the first place, they leave the movement. The Wahhabi movement, however, has continued to have a strong hold on successive generations of Arabs despite obstacles. Twice the Wahhabi movement in the Saudi state was defeated by its enemies, leaving its political and religious leaders dead or taken prisoners. But after each defeat the remaining members of the movement came together, advocating the same fundamentalist teachings with the same conviction and zeal, until they succeeded in reforming a new Islamic state.

Though still rejected by some as an aberration, the Wahhabi movement achieved more of its goals than any other Islamic movement in modern times and is gaining popularity today among Muslims worldwide, thereby influencing other movements. In contemporary Saudi Arabia, Islamic scholars though they differ on certain political issues or Islamic rulings, like Muslim scholars everywhere, have been able to reach a consensus on the fundamentals of faith and method, the like of which is not found in any other part of the Muslim world. Thanks to the Wahhabi movement, Saudi society, though not an ideal Islamic society, is more immune than any other Islamic society to the popular forms of *shirk* (the worshipping of other deities besides God), which the founder of the movement condemned.

The worship of God alone is a fundamental pillar of the whole edifice of Islam and a tenet of supreme importance to the Wahhabi movement. Every Muslim says *la ilaha il-la Allah, Muhammadu-r rasool lu lah*, testifying to the fact that there is no deity worthy of worship except God. Abd al-Wahhab preached that it is not enough to profess the statement verbally, not enough to understand its true meaning, not enough to admit its truth, not even enough to worship none but God; in addition one must deny and reject every other object of worship. One must also abstain from any belief, speech, or act that violates the profession of that fundamental belief.[4] Abd al-Wahhab realized that the faith of most Muslims of his time, including the *ulama* (scholars of religion), did not satisfy all these conditions.[5] Fundamentalists of his persuasion would say the same about many present-day Muslims.

To be a true believer in the Wahhabi-Islamic sense of the word, one must:

1) Believe in God as the only creator and substainer of all things. Since this was accepted by even the idolatrous Arabs before the advent of Muhammad and is accepted by the majority of human beings all over the world, this does not by itself make a person a believer in the sense that all Messengers of God wanted an individual to be.[6]

2) The belief that God alone is worthy of worship, and that no one other than God deserves to be worshipped. This, Abd al-Wahhab explained, is the core of *tawheed*, which all Messengers of God advocated and which caused enmity between them and those who denied it. However, the majority of those who call themselves Muslims, including some in the *ulama*, are ignorant of this and do not satisfy this condition. Although those Muslims would indignantly and emphatically deny such an accusation insisting that they worship none but Allah, they do indeed worship others.

Not only must a true believer worship only God, the believer must worship them in the exact manner prescribed by God's Prophet. This notion refers to the importance of professing Mohammed's Prophethood and agreeing to "obey his orders, to believe what he says, to avoid what he forbids, and not to worship God except in a way He prescribes."[7] The true believer will also believe in the names and attributes which God ascribed to Himself: "To God belongs the names most beautiful; so call Him by them, and leave those who blaspheme His names" (Qur'an, 7:180). A true believer is, therefore, one who takes these names and attributes as they are, without likening them to the attributes of created things (anthropomorphism), and without explaining them metaphorically, a practice which amounts to denying them.[8]

If the believer agrees that only God the Creator is worthy of worship, the crucial question then becomes what does worship consist of? The answer to this is a recurring theme of Abd al-Wahhab's writings. Here are some examples of the feelings and actions that he feels are legitimate expressions of worship, belonging to God alone:

1) Love. It is natural for a person to love many people and many things besides God. But he is not a true believer if he loves anything as much or more than he loves God. The Qur'an says, "There are some people who associate

partners (to God), whom they love as deeply as they love God. But those who believe, love God more deeply (than they love anything else)." Commenting on this verse, Abd al-Wahhab observed that "God stated that they [the so-called believers] love God as they love the ones they took as equal to Him, which means that their love for God was great, but that did not make them Muslims. What then about one who loves the compeer more than He loves God? And what about the one who loves the compeer one, to the exclusion of God?"[9]

2) Fear. The Sheikh counts fear among acts of worship and quotes the Qur'an, "Don't fear them, fear me" (2:150). But this should not be taken to mean that one should not fear anything besides God; rather it should be taken to mean that one should not fear anything as much as or more than one fears God because this would interfere with one's obedience to God. The Qur'an says "Surely we will try you with something of fear and hunger, and diminution of goods and lives and fruits" (2:155)

3) Supplication and invocation. "Call on those whom you claimed (to be gods) apart from Him. They have no power to remove affliction from you or to transfer it. Those they call upon are themselves seeking the means to come to their Lord, which of them shall be nearer; they hope for His mercy, and fear His chastisement. Surely your Lord's chastisement is a thing to beware of" (Qur'an, 17:56-7). Abd al-Wahhab says this is a clear indictment of the associationists who pray to the righteous; this supplication is a form of the major *shirk* and violation of *tawheed*.

4) Obedience. The Qur'an says that some Jews and Christians took their rabbis, priests, and Jesus as lords besides God, whilst they were commanded to worship none but God (9:31). They took them as gods in the sense that they obeyed others and did what God forbade. To obey anyone other than Him is to take another besides God.

5) The Islamic State. Because obedience is owed only to God, Wahhabi Muslims reject the Western secular idea of separation of church and state. Divine commandments are to be obeyed in all situations and at all costs. No one, not a dictator, elected national body, or religious scholar has the right to make legislation that contradicts the Qur'an or the Hadith of the Prophet. To do so is to put oneself in God's place, committing an act of grave *shirk*. The same goes for those who voluntarily obey secular legislation. The Qur'an describes as *taghoot* anyone or anything that is worshipped besides God. Abd al-Wahhab says that there are many *taghoots*, but the five main ones are: a) *sata*, which invites people to worship gods other than God; b) the unjust ruler who distorts God's rulings; c) the one who rules in accordance with laws other than those that God decreed, "be coming, an unbeliever" (5:44); d) the one who claims to know *ghayb* (that which is beyond human senses); and e) the

one who approves of being worshipped like a god. Of these five *taghoot*s three are related to government.

6) Sacrifice. Because animal sacrifice is a form of worship, the slaughtering of animals for the sake of anyone other than God is a form of *shirk*. The Qur'an says to the Prophet, "Pray to your Lord and sacrifice" (108:2). And the Prophet himself says, "May God curse the one who sacrifices for other than God."[10]

All the forms of worship just listed are owed to God and no other. Those who venerate saints in such ways would emphatically deny that they are worshipping them in the same way that they worship God. Rather they would say — as they used to say at the time of the Sheikh and as they are still saying — we know that they are not gods and that the saints do not have any power independent of God, but we turn to them because they have a special place with God; they are our intermediaries to God. Abd al-Wahhab replied by saying this was exactly the argument of the idolatrous Arabs. They claimed that they worshipped idols only so that the idols would "bring them nearer and closer to God" (39:3). "Remember," says the Sheikh, "that the form of *shirk* committed by the associationists whom the Prophet battled against, was that they made supplication to God, but also to the idols and to saints like Jesus and his mother, and to the Angels, saying that they were their intermediaries with God. They did not believe that God, exalted is He, is the one who benefits and harms and disposes [of all affairs.] God stated this about them . . . 'Who provides you out of heaven and earth, or who has power over hearing and sight, and who brings forth the living from the dead or the dead from the living, and who disposes the affair?' They will surely say, 'God'" (10:31).

Some modern critics of Abd al-Wahhab accuse him of being a literalist. To what extent is this true? Certainly the opponents of fundamentalism, whether Christians or Muslims, us the term pejoratively, to condemn the literal method of interpreting scripture. But the method being condemned as literalist is in fact the method that all of us use most of the time to interpret any discourse. We usually interpret what other people say by assigning meaning to their words and expressions in context. It is only after we have interpreted a speaker's discourse in the so-called literalist way that we judge whether what was said was right or wrong, good or bad, appropriate or inappropriate. This process is not peculiar to the so-called fundamentalist interpretation of scripture.

This normal method of interpreting texts, which is literalist, should not be confused with another method that is also sometimes described as literal, and which is indeed irrational. Irrational interpretation isolates the author's words from their context, especially in idiomatic phrases in order to manipulate the meaning. Fundamentalists are usually not accused of this kind of literalism, since their main aim is to understand what the words of God or one of His true Prophets mean, but this method is resorted to by so-called liberals.

So-called liberal interpretation is no more than self deception because although the liberal starts by interpreting scripture in a literal way, when he finds the meaning unacceptable he reinterprets it so as to make it compatible with his personal prejudices or those of his culture. Such a person is only deceiving himself, even if his motive is to make religion acceptable to his contemporaries, because those contemporaries are not accepting the original religion, whether Islam or Christianity or Judaism, but rather accepting a distorted form of it. God warns His Prophet against believing such distortions: "O Messenger! Convey that which was sent down to you from your lord, otherwise you will not be conveying His Message" (Qur'an, 5:67).

In addition to being labeled literalist the Wahhabi movement is also accused of being synonymous with Arabian by some non-Muslim scholars and by modernist Muslims. Whenever they find something in Islamic traditions that they deem unsuitable for modern times, they are prone to say that it is merely a piece of Arab culture that has found its way into Islam through the Arab *ulama*. However, too often what modernists dismiss as merely Arab culture are parts of a culture that the Arabs adopted after the advent of Islam. It is a fact, though it might seem paradoxical, that nothing is more similar to contemporary Western culture than the purely Arab culture that was prevailing before the advent of Islam. It is this culture which Islam condemned as *jahiliya* (ignorance) and which it replaced by a culture based on true moral values. It is the recurrence of this *jahiliya* culture which fundamentalists like Abd al-Wahhab fought against. Abd al-Wahhab's call was not for the deculturalization of Muslims who were not Arabs. Rather, regardless of their ethnic background or nationality, he exhorted all Moslems to obey the words of the Qur'an in a literal sense.

Abd al-Wahhab and his followers, inspired by his Islamic convictions, founded a religious force that not only is accepted in the Arab Peninsula, but also has spread to Muslim communities around the world. Yet the only thing that makes this group of believers any more fundamentalist than any other religious faction, is their belief in God, His words, and the words of His Prophet.

The Holy Ka'aba at Mecca Al-Mukaramah.

Notes

1. In the 1830s and1840s a great deal of excitement was generated in the United States in expectation of the second advent of Christ and an ensuing thousand years of peace (the "millennium"). Further discussion of this can be found in the 1992 *Encyclopedia Britannica.*

2. Alan Bullock, *The Fontana Dictionary of Modern Thought*, 2nd ed., London, 1990.

3. *Fath al Bari*, 1:127.

4. Unless otherwise indicated, the source of all quotations from the Sheikh's writings come from Volume One of the collection of his works, *Mu'alafat ash-Shaykh Muhammad Ibn Abd al-Wahhab*, (Riyadh: Imam Muhammad Ibn Saud Islamic U).

5. Wahhab, 399.

6. Wahhab, 200.

7. Two Qur'an's are used in this article as references, *The Holy Qur'an*, trans. A. Y. Ali, and A. J. Arberry, *The Koran Interpreted.*

8. Sheikh Sulayman ibn abd Allah bin Muhammad ibn abd al-Wahhab, *Taysirul azizil hamid fi sharhi kitabit tawhid.* (Beirut: al Maktabul Islamic, 1988), pp 636, 645-47.

9. Wahhab 25.

10. Wahhab 35.

Women and Saudi Society

by
Anna Marie Weiss-Armush

In 1992 I led a seminar on Saudi and Gulf cuisine at the Smithsonian Institute in Washington, D.C. The presentation was followed by a brief question-and-answer period. I was totally startled to find that only two of the inquiries dealt with the subject of food, that even in the august halls of our nation's capital the public's curiosity was focused on the role of women in the Kingdom. Two women from a not-so-friendly embassy refused to accept my answers and cornered me at a social function later that evening, suggesting that since there were no longer Arabs present, I could tell the truth about how degrading it was to wear the veil, how insufferable it was not to be allowed to drive a car, how repulsive life behind harem walls must have been.

This misunderstanding is reflected in newspaper articles, books, films, and — over and over — in personal experiences. Two Pakistani Muslim friends, one who is the president of the Dallas International Women's Club, recently shared with us their plans to join the haj pilgrimage to Mecca this year. A shocked response came from our vice-president, a well-traveled college professor: "But it's so dangerous for a woman! People are always being killed over there, and then there's that woman who was stoned to death!"

I've grown accustomed to this stereotyped view of the Arab-Muslim world which judge an entire culture on the basis of superficial and relatively insignificant details. Ever since the European Christian Crusades in Jerusalem, the West has tried to frighten its citizens about the Arabs to the point of paralyzing their intellects. We view the Arab-Muslim world through an alien set of Western values, trying to compare their lives to our lives, their women's roles to our women's roles. We dehumanize the value of Arab culture, and we make "Muslims" create a phantom foe.

I no longer hope to find in mainstream books, under chapters entitled "The Shackles of Sex" and "Mysteries of the Harem" anything but the view that women are submissive marginal creatures huddled in black veils. Most of the journalists and authors do not speak Arabic and lived only briefly on the margins of the Saudi culture. Their interest is in marketing titles, in selling the film rights, in making money. Stories like *Not Without My Daughter* bring in big bucks. The excellent studies written by women like Elizabeth Fernea, Fatima Mernissi, and Soraya Al-Torki sell fewer copies and generate lower royalties.

Comparative Values

For me a realization of the complex situation began the day I shared with colleagues the news that I was planning to marry an Syrian. "HOW COULD YOU?!" responded our secretary, her shocked face twisted with a display of repugnance.

We were married by a Catholic priest in a ceremony that I wrote, with an imam reciting verses from the Qur'an and a rabbi friend reading from The Book of Ruth. "Wherever you go, I will go," I told my husband. "Take me anywhere, but please, not to Saudi Arabia." Even then we believed the dreadful rumors about the Kingdom.

A year later, in 1976, eight months pregnant, I arrived in Jeddah. My husband accepted a job offer, and we decided to move, but only for three years. Our plan was to save a bit of money and return once our son was of nursery school age.

To clarify my position, I should mention that I am neither a journalist, seeking to sell a shocking story to her editor, nor an anthropologist documenting an unusual way of life. Nor have I converted to Islam, as Muslim men may marry women "of the Book," that is, Jews, Christians, or Muslims who worship the same monotheistic God. I have always considered myself a feminist, and my husband would certainly categorize me as an activist. From 1976 to 1987 my strategy was simply to confess my ignorance to family, friends, and neighbors, and ask them to teach me how to be the wife of a Arab-Muslim.

And their counsel was unceasing. My Syrian mother-in-law taught me how to fulfill my domestic responsibilities, filling my husband's stomach with delicious food and my children's hearts with modesty, respect, and an awareness of their responsibilities to the family. Saudi friends demonstrated the generous art of giving gifts to cement relationships of trust. Countless numbers of taxi drivers asked me if I had become a Muslim and advised me that I would find the answers in The Book. And the Mixed Nuts, an informal support group of mostly-American women married to Saudis and other Arabs, helped me surmount cultural enigmas and obstacles, the interminable frictions and confrontations of daily life.

As we Mixed Nuts discussed our new environment, it became clear to me that we were operating under a set of cultural values completely different from those of our lands of origin. We had entered a society in which our grandmothers would be more at ease than they would in suburban America today.

Studies show that the prime guiding value of American life is not "freedom", as I am frequently told by lower elementary students. By sixth grade our children realize that what is most important in this country is money. In contrast, Saudis regard their families of major significance, followed by religion, and then human relations. Family support has always been indispensable in the unpredictable world of the Middle East, and the importance of family is expressed in the rich terminology of the region. The Arab family offers a totality of financial, educational, and social services: relatives employ family members, aunts seek out husbands for their nieces, and the middle aged provide care for the elderly and unmarried females. Those in need of loans or advice turn to their kin, as do those seeking *wasta* ("connections") to uncover places in good schools or scarce airline seats at *Eid* time.

The Arab family provides emotional and financial security for each of its members under a warm protective blanket of love. There are no homeless wandering the streets of Jeddah, no homes for the unwanted elderly or handicapped. Orphanages are almost an anomaly. Honoring family obligations is not only a cultural ideal but also a religious duty, and man's responsibility to support his household extends to any family dependents who have no one else to look after them. Most Saudi households include female relatives not employed the household, even old family friends, widowed neighbors, or elderly former servants.

Traditionally, all men of a family worked together in joint ventures, and the expenditures of each member and each part of the family were defrayed from the common pot. Extended families lived in one large building housing father with his married sons and their wives and children. Until ten years ago, my husband's family still shared this type of housing arrangement. Older generation women like my mother-in-law deferred to their husbands in every way and were secluded. Their social world was widened through a network of friendships that played an important role in their lives. Even today these organized patterns of female visits provide Saudi women with vital information about community events, possible marriage partners, etc.

Today, young couples usually find the differences in experiences, education, and values that exist between the generations challenging, and there is a general trend away from the extended family toward the nuclear family. When families still live together, there are likely to be separate entrances and exits, with reduced contact between the married couple and their parents. Very popular, especially among Saudi couples of my age ("middle generation" in anthropological terminology), are family compounds where father and sons each live in private homes called villas, but with shared gardens. Or a father may own a valuable piece of land on which he builds a row of identical villas, one for himself and one for each son or daughter. Most adult children prefer to live close to their parents.

The benefits of close family ties should be obvious to us, but to my American friends who protest that their families are close, too, I reply that it is not at all the same. The Arab family is always there for each other in an unequaled circle of affection. Children benefit from the full devotion of their mothers during their early years but also from the love and guidance of doting aunts and uncles. In contrast to the "Me! Now!" demands of this culture, Arab adults and children learn to subordinate their personal wishes to those of the head of the family. From a young age they learn to conform and to obey and honor their elders. In the traditional system, innovation and individuality are discouraged because they might threaten the authority of the leader and the cohesiveness of the group.

In Saudi Arabia, the new pattern for educated young married couples who have greater contact with the outside world than their parents is to spend more time together and to engage in more joint decisions. Many young wives understandably prefer to be autonomous from their mother-in-law. They monitor household activities, control the budget, and elect to act as companions to their husbands and teachers-mothers for their children after school rather than build the extensive circle of friendships that their mothers relied on.

Women in Islam

Within the family, as well as in every other facet of Arab life, the Qur'an is a comforting cradle, a grounding device, "a compass in a universe of ever-expanding horizons."[1] Islam is more than a religious structure. It is a holistic approach to the world and to every aspect of everyday life. Every detail is covered, from manners to hygiene, to business and family relations. Most significantly, its creed proposes a new system of equality in daily social life.

In pre-Islamic times, the days of the *Jahiliya*, many tribal orders believed that women and their wealth were part of the inherited goods. In these tribes sons would inherit the family's women upon their father's death. Wives were purchased, and female captives were considered part of a warrior's booty for fighting in battle.

Islam was born in the arms of a woman when the prophet Muhammed received his first revelation. It was to his wife Khadija, not to a male friend, that the Prophet turned for comfort and support. Muhammed's message radically challenged the paternalistic attitudes of the *Jahiliya*.

In Islam, the financial details of society's economic responsibility to women are clearly enumerated: husbands must support their wives to a level similar to that which they received in their fathers' houses. At a time when European women turned their fortunes over to their husbands on the wedding day, Muslim women were declared financially independent. They are guaranteed the right to hold their own wealth, run their own businesses or hold jobs, and spend and invest their money as they like.

The Qur'an also introduced the revolutionary dogma that men and women are equal in the eyes of God and that the superior individual is the "most God-fearing of you".[2] So appealing was the concept of justice and equality that women of the peninsular flocked to join Muhammed's band of followers, even if it meant leaving their non-believing husbands behind.

In those days men and women mixed freely and used to gather every evening to discuss their new faith. Frequently social problems and questions were submitted to the Prophet, and his companions would await a clarification from heaven. When his wife Um Salama asked Muhammed why female believers were not specifically mentioned in the book, God responded in the following way:

"Men who surrender unto Allah, and women who surrender,
and men who believe and women who believe,
and men who obey and women who obey,
and men who speak the truth and women who speak the truth, (...)
Allah has prepared for them forgiveness and a vast reward." (33-35)

The answer was clear. Female and male members of the community are equal. Faith and actions, not one's sex, determine his reward.

During the Prophet's time, women prayed in the mosques, did not veil, and were not secluded. The dynamic ladies of early Islam, it seems to me, are excellent role models for today's Muslim women. Muhammed's first wife, Khadija, was an imposingly successful trader, who sent a maidservant to propose marriage to him, her younger employee. The poet laureate of the tribes during Muhammed's time, a woman named Al-Khansa, followed her sons to battle seated in her camel litter and reciting verses exhorting men and women to fight on for Islam.

Many women are remembered for their wit and sharp minds. The elegant and beautiful daughter of the Prophet's cousin Ali, Sukayna married four times. One of her husbands, the caliph's grandson, promised in their marriage contract never to divorce her, nor touch another woman, nor contradict her in anything, nor refuse anything she wished, and when he broke his word she sued him in the Islamic courts in a violent confrontation. A'isha Bint Talha, granddaughter of the first caliph, refused her husband's command to veil herself, saying that if God had honored her with beauty, there was no shame in people looking upon her face.

One of my personal favorites among these remarkable women in Walladah bint al Mustakfi, an eleventh century Andalusian poetess, daughter through an Ethiopian slave mother to a degenerate caliph who was reduced to poverty by excessive gastronomic and sexual adventures. Refusing to veil or marry,

Walladah opened a brilliant salon to which people of letters, both men and women, flocked to discuss poetry, music, and the arts. On her right sleeve was embroidered the verse "I am, by God, fit for high positions, and am going my way, with pride!"

The Prophet himself was very fond of women, and enjoyed their intellect, their beauty, and their company. "The best among you are those who are good to their womenfolk," he said, and when asked who he loved most in the world, he responded his young wife A'isha. His companions pressed for a better answer and asked whom he loved best among men. "Abu Bakr, the father of my beloved," he answered.

This radical new view of women as not appreciated by all of the Prophet's companions, many of whom preferred the dominating machismo of the *Jahilya*. After the Prophet's death, when the Islamic Empire swept east and west across much of the world, the social status of women began to change. Men ingeniously reinterpreted some of Muhammed's relevations, to add an Islamic stamp of approval to the growing decadence of the caliphates. Certain verses of scripture, which were previously an open door, were transformed into a barrier.

The second caliph, Umar, favorite of the Prophet and a charismatic exemplary leader, felt that Islam's changes should be limited to the spiritual life of women. Notoriously anti-women, Umar supported men who feared women's autonomy, and he said, "It is a fact that all the truths, misfortunes and woes which befall men come from women."

The Prophet is considered "the fine example" for every Muslim, but his followers continued to distort the message by submitting false *hadiths*, saying attributed to Muhammed, to support their position. For example, Al Bukhari, a leading collector of *hadith*, reported that the Prophet said, "Three things bring bad luck: house, woman and horse." Muhammed's favorite wife A'isha corrected him, claiming that the Prophet had said "May Allah refute the Jews, they say three things bring bad luck . . .," but her comments were not recorded in Al-Bukhari's volumes.

Twenty five years after the event, Abu Bakr, a freed slave turned prosperous Muslim, extricated him from a political dispute by opportunely recalling that the Prophet had said, "Those who entrust their affairs to a woman will never know prosperity." A'isha, then an Islamic judge, challenged these reported quotations and her co-wives supported her because they were conscious of the implications. Time after time they demonstrated that they were taken out of context or misquoted, or the outright inventions of women-hating men. But when the collections of authentic hadiths were published, the women's views were not always included.

The *Hijab*, Veils and Harems

It was in Persia and Christian Byzantium that the harem, head covering, and face veil originated, and these symbols of luxury and aristocracy were absorbed by the invading Bedouin, along with local chauvinistic attitudes as seen in the Persian saying, "Take a wife every year, friend, since a used calendar is not really of much value."[3]

An element of great mystery to the West, the veil or *abaya* is no more than a basic unshaped square garment common to traditional societies across the world. Its use varies according to the situation, the location, and the individuals involved. It is also a symbol of woman's mystery and charm. Those outside the impenetrable darkness of *abaya* and veil cannot ever penetrate the autonomous and self-sufficient world of women, while properly dressed women move freely through the men's world, seeing without being seen.

Your black veil entices me
Opens me to the hunger of desire and envelopes me
It hides the sun behind it
And conceals the radiant moon and the breaking dawn behind it
And almost divulges its light behind the night.[4]

Just as swim suits belonged around the pool, and silk dresses were correct attire for Saudi parties, I found the *abaya* to be the appropriate covering for most public activities. The perfect equalizer, it was lightweight and cool, and could be thrown over just about any outfit.

The Qur'anic injunctions on modesty are clearly directed to both men and women: "Tell believers to avert their glances and to guard their private parts. . . God is informed about anything they do" (24:30). By wearing the abaya I was marked as a modest woman, and all Muslim men were required to treat me with appropriate respect and courtesy: "O Prophet, tell your wives and daughters and the women of the believers to draw upon their over-garments. That is more appropriate so that they may be recognized and not molested. (33:59)

Properly covered, I was never afraid to ride in a Saudi taxi or to walk the streets alone at night, or to carry large sums of cash. The *abaya* was my key to a very practical and real freedom.

I wish I could say the same about other countries I have visited. A lone woman in most parts of the world is believed to be looking for male attention. When I visited Mexico, my path was followed by smacking lips, hoots, slurps, and loud kissing noises, and excursions into crowded buses and public spaces resulted in humiliating fondling, squeezing, and poking. Even Muslim countries are not completely free from minor exhibitions of some males' lack of self-control. But during the years in Saudi Arabia that I wore the *abaya* I was free from the fear of thieves and molesters, free to explore the fascinating land around me.

Ironic as it may seem to a Westerner, I also discovered that women's freedom was increased by the seclusion presented by our walled villas. These harem walls were not at all claustrophobic or mysterious as one would imagined: window shutters and blinds were left open all day long, filling our spacious rooms with bright desert sunlight, and during the winter, we didn't fear to sleep with the windows wide open. The children could play in our yard safely, without apprehension, while I worked inside the house. It was easy for me to see that for a poor woman who toiled in the scorching sun, it was a lifetime dream to sit behind the protective walls of her home sipping tea with the ladies of the neighborhood.

Muslims sincerely believe that the primary job of a woman is to raise her children and create a secure and peaceful atmosphere in the home. Their responsibility is considered no less valuable than the one performed by men. This belief leaves women in control of the family and everything that is held most valuable in Muslim culture. Muslim men are required by the Qur'an to bear the financial burden and he must struggle in the public arena. This separation of responsibilities ensures the integrity and stability of the family, which is the primary goal of Muslim society.

In practical terms, this "harem mentality" meant that my husband took over a long list of chores that I handle here in the States. Most Arab men would, for example go out to the vegetables and the meat markets and drive the children to school. Segregation also makes women nearly autonomous, conducting their daily lives with other women independently of men. This independence is reinforced by Arab men's expressed desire not to be bothered by the small details and problems of domestic life. So women become the course of power, setting higher and broader goals than simple equality with men.

Islam and Sex

Islamic thought also introduced a striking new attitude toward sex. In Christianity, Eve's sexual exploration is punished by expulsion from Paradise.[5] During eight years of Catholic education the nuns taught me that chastity is noble and that the purpose of sexual activity is procreation. Sex in Christianity is considered animal-like and anti-civilization. The soul strives to triumph over the flesh.

In contrast, Islam recommends sexual satisfaction; it is understood that people cannot reach their full potential of work, creativity, or spiritual understanding if they are frustrated by unfulfilled sexual desires. One of Muhammed's disciples even made it a habit to have sexual intercourse before the important evening prayer, to ensure that his mind would be clear and able to concentrate fully on the greatness of God. Some theologians insist that God gave mankind sex to provide a taste of the pleasures the righteous will enjoy in paradise. The Andalusian physican Ibn Sina (called Avicenna in the West) recognized in the seventh century that sexual needs were not weaknesses of the flesh, but rather natural states which had to be satisfied in order to maintain psychological and physical health. Islam's liberal, naturalistic view of sexuality includes the Prophet's insistence on foreplay and satisfaction for the woman:

"You must not throw yourselves on your wives, as beasts do. Before you join with your wife in intercourse, let there be a message running backwards and forwards between you and her." And his followers asked, 'What message?' 'A message of kisses and tender words,' he replied. (Ihya Quloum El Dinei 734.)

Nevertheless, Islam inherited Judaic patriarchal values and its condemnation of Eve. To avoid sin brought on by a passionate nature, Islam strongly encourages men to marry. The Prophet told his followers, "Marry and multiply." Adds theologian Al-Ghazali, "Since Allah has revealed his secret to us, and has instructed us clearly what to do, refraining from marriage is like refusing to plough the earth, and wasting the seed. It means leaving the useful tool which Allah has created for us idle" (169). Marriage, therefore, keeps men and women from committing sins of passion inspired by the devil.

Marriage in Islam is not a holy sacrament whose bonds cannot be severed, but rather is viewed as a legal contract between man and woman. Arab couples enter marriage with fewer idealistic or romantic expectations. Even more than companionship and love, men and women seek financial security, social status, and children in their unions. In real terms, marriage is a contract between two families or clans, rather than between two individuals.

In a segregated society, opportunities to meet potential mates are naturally severely limited, and when women are veiled, men may never see the faces of females outside their immediate family group. Consequently, even though women in the days of early Islam interacted with men and often were the ones to propose marriage, today a young man usually relies on his mother or other female relatives to make enquiries among their social circle and in their neighborhood about daughters of marriageable age.[6] Young men and women accept this system as prudent because they realize that their parents love them and want the best for them.

To a Westerner, arranged marriages may seem primitive and insensitive, yet I see many advantages in such an approach. Certainly in our society, where marriage is left to the whims of teenage attachments and sexual attraction, divorce rates in the United States (50%) attests to the American system's failure. Middle Eastern girls do not find themselves dressing provocatively, playing "the dumb blond," flirting and stifling their brightness in school, or giving sexual favors simply to attract and keep a young man's attention. Nor do attractive, sensitive women who have missed their chance in the mating ground of college find themselves isolated from the marriage market, without male companionship, unless they are willing to frequent singles bars.

In the Muslim world, the system actually works to the young women's advantage: every girl whose female relatives undertake to find her a husband, will be married. Even homely, disabled, or not-so-bright girls are wed without further ado. And if the parents take their time to find a compatible mate, rather than giving their daughter to the first man who asks for her hand, the marriage is usually remarkably successful because it is based on mutual respect rather than unrealistic goals.

Divorce, which according to the Prophet is "the most hated of all things permissible," is a last resort which is usually worked out amicably by the two clans involved. Divorce is not an admission of mistaken judgement or a sign of personal failure. Children suffer far less than in the West because they have been raised, to a great extent, by the collective family rather than by a parent whom will be losing.

Polygamy served the needs of past generations of women, assuring that no virtuous woman would remain unattached and unprotected. After the death of Muhammed's first wife, Khadija, he married orphaned girls and widows to show his followers that their duty lay in shielding and sheltering all unprotected women. He firmly suggested that second wives be only widows with children and forbade his daughter's husband (who was also his cousin) to take a second wife, saying that what caused pain to his daughter grieved him as well. Polygamy was also preferable to the plagues of adultery and illegitimate children that existed in the Arabian peninsula during the Jahiliya.

In the "old days," which screeched to a halt after the oil boom of 1973, families were large, and polygamy was not uncommon, as numerous sons represented social security and health insurance to the parents. Polygamy is definitely out of fashion these days, for a combination of reasons. The current high standard of living in the Gulf makes compliance with the Qur'an's law to treat each wife equally a very expensive proposition.[7]

Education Opens the Door

It is hard to imagine that there were only thirteen female students in the first graduating class in 1970 at Jeddah's Abdul Aziz University. The total female literacy rate at that time was 4%, and most girls in the Kingdom did not attend school, other than through a Qur'anic institution which taught them to read the holy scriptures. Families who valued female education would either bring a governess from Syria or Lebanon, or send their daughter off to school in Cairo or Beirut.

King Faisal's heroic wife Iffat changed all of that. An expert politician devoted to expanding the horizons of Saudi women, Iffat pushed for educational opportunities under the banner of Islam. By 1960, she had set up a national committee on female education, and schools for girls began to open around the country. Religious leaders found it difficult to resist her argument that Islamic instruction would produce better mothers and homemakers, which would, in turn, improve the spiritual formation of future generations. After all, both male and female Muslims are under equal obligation to read the Qur'an and determine the true intent of its words. And a famous *hadith* recalls the Prophet saying "Seek knowledge, even unto China."

In the early 1980's, a new school was being opened every day. By 1986, 12,253 women were graduating from Saudi institutions of higher learning. Women continue to outshine their brothers on the national exams, as the demand for female education surges. Numbers of female students in higher education grew by 7.1% in 1986, while there was an increase of 19.4% for women. Twenty-two percent of university faculty are women. Many women return to school after having several children.

Separate Societies

Saudi society is actually two societies, one of women and a parallel world of men. Although men and women may interact in the marketplace, as a general rule they are only infrequently in direct physical contact with men. The separate-but-equal institutions which have developed to serve women exemplify ways in which elements of Western technological progress can successfully be incorporated into a system of traditional values.

Unfortunately, just as an American's cultural bias often causes her or him to place exaggerated emphasis on the position of women in Saudi Arabian society, he or she also tends to misinterpret the pattern of these dual institutions and services, which have developed to meet necessity and public demand. Segregated exercise clubs, tailoring establishments and beauty salons, and even the SAPTCO bus compartments are severely criticized by Westerners. But to Arab women who see cultural limitations on education, employment, and personal expression so suddenly lifted, these changes are hardly superficial.

Yes, I, too, was amused when I heard about female gynecologists and pediatricians and hospitals for women run by women. But the truth is that many women are still uncomfortable in integrated public places. Perhaps it is a sign of our own sexual prejudice that we assume most doctors to be male, and criticize a society which supports clinics run by women for women. Is it possible that Saudi Arabia's push to develop facilities to serve the specific needs of women puts it in the vanguard of the feminist movement?

Saudi women have met great success in the fields of journalism, banking, and education. As self-made women like Dr. Aminal Shakir, editor in chief of *Sayyidati*, tell the stories of their struggle, the debate on working women continues openly in the daily newspapers. Now that education has opened many doors, the Saudi system of dual institutions means that women have opportunities to develop their talents in relatively sheltered situations. It is a great advantage to women that their society encourages them to search for their identities and strive to reach their potential without fear of male competition or adverse criticism. They are autonomous within their own sphere, no longer assuming the inferior role conferred on them by male relatives or associates.

Today's Saudi woman operates under a lower stress level than her Western counterpart because she has the support of her extended family, household help, and a more gracious business or work environment in which to develop her potential. For the vast number of women working in the field of education, the Ministry of Education has opened one nursery to serve every two schools. Transportation to work is usually provided, and teachers are posted to schools near their homes. In addition, most women live in clusters of houses owned by members of the extended family or in the same neighborhood as their relatives, which eases the burden of child-care.

Most Saudi women are employed by the government and feel they are providing a service to the public and the nation. They are highly committed professional women, working as teachers, surgeons, social workers, and lab technicians. Positions of low social status reserved for women in the West (secretaries, sales clerks, factory workers) are filled by men, usually imported labor. Saudi women therefore avoid dead-end jobs that put them on public display and those lacking social prestige. While working women in other Arab countries do so out of economic necessity, Saudi women tend to work more for intellectual satisfaction and personal fulfillment, or as a means of building up wider social networks.

With Saudi women holding at least 40% of the country's wealth, many women have opened businesses and factories, either using male employees to operate them or hiring other women to work in a "women only" establishment. Atidal Muhammed Saleen was one of the first women to operate a major Saudi business enterprise. In 1971, suddenly a widow with several children and a tiny infant, she decided to forge ahead and try to keep her husband's company afloat. Disregarding the protestations of others in the community, who complained that it was reprehensible for a woman to negotiate contracts and supervise a company because it entailed face-to-face contact with men, Atidal managed to meet the contractual obligations for maintenance on Aramco's buildings at the Petromin complex. Known for their talent in the marketplace, Saudi women like Atidal continue to live up to their entrepreneurial families' reputations, finding ambitious new ways to make their assets grow.

Frequently, a Saudi woman will have developed new perspectives after exposure to Western culture and returned to become a pioneer in her field. Safiya Benzagar, a Jeddite who had been raised abroad, was for many years the only recognized Saudi artist. Safiya enjoyed her family's complete support, and they arranged for public exhibitions of her work. Safiya believes that it is precisely because of her years in Cairo and England that her native country's culture and tradition appeared fascinatingly fresh to her, and she decided to focus on preserving her Saudi heritage through her art.

Like other expatriate women, I appreciate the leisure time that permitted me to develop new skill and explore new fields. But even more important, I recognized that my numerous successes were due, at least in part, to a system which encouraged women to met the needs of women, and to the lack of male interference in women's affairs.

Yes, I wore the veil. And I wrote *Arabian Cuisine*. And I traveled to every major city in the Kingdom to lecture to women on Arab culture and traditions. I owned a boutique of fine Arabian jewelry and clothing, and I organized and presented fashion shows for women's groups. I was a columnist for both the *Arab News* and the *Saudi Gazette*. My television series for Saudi Channel 2 was so well-received that I was asked to take over the weekly "magazine" show. Had I remained in the States there is no doubt that I would have remained cubbyholed in a teaching position, trying to balance family and work. It is indeed a paradox that, like me, many Muslim women own their successful careers to Islamic law, the harem tradition, and the ancient concept of honor.

Sex Role Conflicts

If Saudi women find that existing social patterns and public facilities make combining work, family, and personal life quite feasible, there still remain many issues of self-definition to be resolved. The older generation, these women's mothers, understood the parameters of their lives and learned to exploit their roles, but women of the middle and younger generations are sometimes perplexed. In order to refute the appalling misrepresentation of facts presented by the Western media, I think it is essential for us to listen to the true comments and complaints of Arab women.

American feminists protest the double standard, sexual harassment, the glass ceiling in employment. Are Saudi women longing to throw off the *abaya*, grab their car keys, and drive off into the desert sunset? Far from it! They consider themselves far more fortunate than we are. And there is no doubt in my mind that they are far more fortunate than their Arab sisters in Syria, Egypt, and Morocco. Nor do Saudi women disapprove, as Americans would expect, of the restrictions of a conservative society. Our Saudi and Muslim sisters are primarily concerned with the same problems we face in this country: jobs, children, divorce . . . and relations with their husbands.

"Let's not bother the men about this," suggest Talaat, a psychiatrist who was working on a charitable project with me. "If we want to get anything done, we'd better handle it ourselves. You know how our men are when it comes to our undertakings."

Amina, president of a Muslim women's association, thinks men are operating under amnesia, still warping the message of the Qu'ran. "I think men are afraid of us because we are stronger and more effective. So they find excuses to interfere, to control, to assert their power. How very convenient it is for them to relegate women again to the status of servants."

Leila complains that her husband doesn't fulfill his responsibilities because when she has essential social visits to make (for the birth of a child or a friend's wedding) he is always too tired to drive her. "If our society doesn't permit women to drive and my husband doesn't want to hire a driver, he shouldn't always expect to relax at home while I must beg a relative for a ride."

Jihan is a professional who is in charge of every minute detail of her family's financial life, but in front of guests her husband postures to impress them with his masculine control. "Didn't you prepare the watermelon?!" "What's the matter with you? No yoghurt for the rice?" "Why did you cook this? Did you actually think we'd like it?"

Assia, a vibrant young Saudi with a PhD. from Stanford, dresses very modestly but without the *abaya*. She is willing to face the fury that this prompts from some perfect strangers who accuse her of immorality. She is also irate at letters written by macho extremists to a national newspaper which say that "it is better to keep food and women covered" and "Man is meant to rule, woman to be ruled!" as quoted in *The Arab News*. Assia thinks that the social situation will continue to develop as women are more educated and are aware of their Islamic rights.

Fawziyya Abu Khalid, a Saudi poet, claims that men are selfish and weak, with a backbone that is nothing "but a pillar of fog frozen in the Levantine mirror of Narcissus." Fawziyya faults the patriarchal system for producing men who claim to support women's rights but are really pimps "hailing the virtues of the fruits of the Fertile Crescent."

Fatima Mernissi, a brilliant North African sociologist reminds us that "If women's rights are a problem for some modern Muslim men, it is neither because of the Qur'an nor the Prophet nor the Islamic tradition, but simply because those rights conflict with the interest of a male elite."[8]

Freedom

I continue to be amazed that the most common question, often the only question American friends, relatives, strangers, even publishers and editors ask me about Saudi Arabia is "How could you, a woman, stand it in such a place, where you have no freedom?"

The truth is that our move required an extraordinary cultural adjustment. Yes, it was difficult at first, just as it would be if I moved to Brownsville or New York City. But in fact, American women who lived in the Kingdom for more than three years almost invariably reply that they love it and wish they had never left.

How is it possible that liberated Western women enjoy living in a place where women have "no freedom?" The answer must be related to one's definition of "freedom," or, perhaps, with the definition of "woman."

After years of addressing American audiences of all ages and types, it appears to me that lack of "freedom" in Saudi Arabia is equated with wearing the veil and the prohibition against women driving. These are two insignificant elements of the social system which certainly do not reflect the complex issues facing women in that country or across the world. My freedom, in fact, was increased, not diminished, by wearing a black cloak. Restrictions on driving, irritating though they may be, do not reduce freedom, either. Freedom, I discovered, is not a physical substance, measured in veils and drivers' licenses, but rather an intangible substance of the spirit. It is the soul's ability to soar high above the lackluster world in search of fulfillment and inner peace.

For another perspective, I asked Maureen Crane, an American Aramco employee dependent who was forced to take refuge in Dallas during the Gulf conflict, how she would respond to the questions about freedom. "In the Kingdom," Maureen responded, "a basic respect and appreciation of human life exists. People become an exciting resource, and there is time to enjoy friendships. The basic freedoms I was taught in my youth have been immeasurably amplified there, while life in America has become a series of obstacles to my physical and emotional well-being. In Dallas, I cannot open my door, nor walk at night, nor let my child play outside. America's unlimited freedom has produced a bunch of crazies hyped on drugs to plague us. There is no respect for humanity here, no control of your own life. How am I free if I must live in fear?"

Most Westerners are convinced that Middle Eastern women suffer a loss of personal freedom. Our Arab friends are equally certain that they have an advantage. "We are happy. We have more freedom than you" is the usual comment. In the Muslim world, conformity is external and often superficial, but it is unfair to assume that life in the private and pubic spheres is identical.

In the United States, we tout freedom as our principal cultural value and heritage, and we live under the illusion that we are free and independent beings. True, ours is a land of great opportunity, but the pursuit of money has become more vivid, more intense than any other aspiration. We have lots of material things, but no time, which limits the inner space in which to search for some higher meaning to life. In Saudi, not only were our spirits free, not only did we encourage each other to challenge and expand our personal and social horizons, but the system provided support which reinforced that liberty and permitted us to seek more elevated goals. In America, survival, rather than freedom, is one's priority. I feel trapped, restricted, and controlled by the turbulent economic and social forces of my environment. There is no time to visit friends or explore new endeavors and not even enough time to dedicate to my family. "Equality," under the banner of sexual liberation, has proved to be a contemporary tyranny.

The principle challenge to the Arab and Muslim world today is in learning how to integrate Western technological information without losing its heritage of Muslim values. It is impossible to expect a culture to face issues in one or two generations which the West took generations to digest. One cannot eliminate, at the stroke of a pen, customs practices for centuries without being aware that the arrow of time, which now speeds toward the future, might possibly sink, wounded, back toward a comforting and protected past.

It is a grave error to assume, as most Americans do, that Saudi women are dutifully shuffling four steps behind their husbands, shrouded in black, mute, obliging, tragically condemned to a life of subservience. The young women of Saudi Arabia continue to follow the vibrant examples set by A'isha, Sukayna, and Um-Salama, and not the memory of the harem slave.

Notes

1. Fatima Mernissi, *Beyond the Veil: Male-Female Dynamics in Modern Muslim Society*, Bloomington: Indiana U P, 1987): xi.

2. Mernissi 49.

3. From the Persian poet Sa'di, who died in 1292.

4. From a poem by Yemeni poet Muhammad al Sharafi, who finds inspiration in the veil because it symbolically expresses the contradictions of Arab culture in the peninsula today.

5. In Islam, both Adam and Eve are seen as responsible for their banishment.

6. Although Muslim men do not usually marry until they are financially able to set up a household, society understands that without sexual outlets they may be drawn toward sin. Consequently, a young man often receives financial aid from his father and mother that enables him to get married.

7. "If you fear that you will be able to do justice to the orphan girls by taking them in marriage, then marry women of your choice from among the other women, two or three, or four. But if you shall not be able to keep equality amongst your wives, then marry only one" (4:3). Also, "You are never able to be fair and just as between women" (4:129).

8. Soraya Altorki, *Women in Saudi Arabia: Idealogy and Behavior Among the Elite*, (New York: Columbia U P, 1986): ix.

Epilogue

by
Richard Bianchi

Saudi Arabia: Tradition and Transition presents a forum where the religious and cultural values that shape Saudi Arabia, a country whose survival is of extreme significance to the United States, is presented to American reader. The Kingdom is too often perceived to hold great mystery and parity. Yet, upon closer examination, the Kingdom exhibits diversity and vitality based on its Islamic heritage and Arabian culture. The influence of rapid, oil-financed modernization has obviously added new dimensions to Saudi society, but rather than give up their culture for the purchase of Western lifestyles, the Saudi populace has chosen to create a pattern of development that preserves their traditions. This has allowed the Kingdom to maintain a stable cultural environment for its people.

With this collection we have tried to address American misperceptions about Saudi Arabs. Too many people believe, for example, that the Kingdom has only played a significant role in world politics since the 1973 Oil Embargo. In fact, however, the people of the Arabian peninsula have displayed significant influence in the international arena for centuries.

This is one of many misconceptions people in the West often have about Saudi Arabia. After you have read our collection, we hope you will reconsider your reactions to the following questions and answers.

1. When does the history of Saudi Arabia begin: After the 1973 Oil Embargo, unification of the Kingdom in 1932 by King Abdulaziz Al-Saud, after World War II or in the eighteenth century?

2. What is Islamic Fundamentalism? What function does religion play in Saudi Arabia and who was Sheikh Mohammed bin adb al-Wahhab? How does Islamic Fundamentalism compare with other fundamentalist religious movements?

3. What is the comparative status of Saudi women to American women? What role do women play in the Saudi society work force?

4. What was the Arabian peninsula like thousands of years ago? Archaeologists have found evidence in Saudi Arabia that provides deep insights into the history of ancient civilizations. How does this compare to the archaeology of the United States, which is still a very young country?

5. How has the discovery of oil affected the economy of Saudi Arabia? How have King Faisal's five year economic development plans helped build Saudi Arabia's infrastructure. How has Saudi Arabia expanded its economy beyond the petroleum industry? Does Saudi Arabia have a diversified economy?

6. What are the major forces that influence the Arabian Peninsula? How has religion, notions of Westernization, and petroleum impacted the history and growth of the Saudi Kingdom?

7. How do Saudi Arabs preserve and honor their traditions and folk history today? Besides their religious practices, what traditions do the Saudi people celebrate and hold dear to their hearts?

It is our goal to promote greater understanding by Americans about a nation that has been long shrouded in prejudice. The Kingdom of Saudi Arabia is a land of great diversity ranging from the bedouin shepherd family in the desert to the city dwellers in large metropolitan areas. The presence of a strong religious traditions and a rich cultural heritage endures the ever changing, modernizing socio-economic structure. At the same time, centuries-old principles and values have not been sacrificed in the wake of massive infrastructure construction, making Saudi Arabia a fascinating case study of a society whose traditions are in transition. We hope you have enjoyed reading our book.

SELECTED BIBLIOGRAPHY

Al-Farsy, Fouad. *Modernity and Tradition: The Saudi Equation*. London: Kegan Paul International, 1990.

Al-Suhrawardy, Allama Sir Abdullah Al-Mamun. *The Sayings of Muhammed*. New York: Citadel Press, 1938.

Alghafis, Ali N. *Universities in Saudi Arabia: Their Role in Science, Technology, and Development*. Lanham: University Press of America, 1992.

Altorki, Soraya and Donald P. Cole. *Arabian Oasis City: The Transformation of 'Unayzah*. Austin: University of Texas Press, 1989.

Altorki, Soraya. *Women in Saudi Arabia: Idealogy and Behavior Among the Elite*. New York: Columbia University Press, 1986.

Atiya, Nayra. Khul-Khaal. *Five Egyptian Women Tell Their Stories*. New York: Syracuse University Press, 1982.

Azzam, Henry T. *The Gulf Economies in Transition*. New York: St. Martin's Press, 1988.

Beck, Lois and Nikki Keddie. *Women in the Muslim World*. Cambridge: Harvard University Press, 1978.

Bogary, Hamza, trans. by Olive Kenny and Jeremy Reed. *The Sheltered Quarter: A Tale of a Boyhood in Mecca*. Austin: University of Texas Press, 1991.

Boullata, Kamal. *Women of the Fertile Crescent*. Washington, DC: Three Continents Press, 1978.

Devine, Elizabeth and Nancy L. Braganti. *The Travelers' Guide to Middle Eastern and North African Customs and Manners*. New York: St. Martin's Press, 1991.

El Ghazali, *Abou Hamil. Ihya Ouloum El Dinej*. Cairo: Dar El Shabb Publishers, 1970.

Esposito, John L. *Women in Muslim Family Law*. New York: Syracuse University Press, 1982.

Fernea, Elizabeth Warnock and Basima Qattan Bezirgan. *Middle Eastern Muslim Women Speak*. Austin: University of Texas Press, 1977.

Fernea, Elizabeth Warnock. *Women and the Family in the Middle East: New Voices of Change*. Austin: University of Texas Press, 1985.

Heller, Mark and Nadav Safran. *The New Middle Class and Regime Stability in Saudi Arabia*. Cambridge, MA: Center for Middle Eastern Studies, Harvard University, 1985.

Jayyusi, Salma Khadra. *The Literature of Modern Arabia*. Austin: University of Texas Press, 1988.

Kostiner, Joseph. *The Making of Saudi Arabia, 1916-1936: From Chieftancy to Monarchical State*. New York: Oxford University Press, 1993.

Makhlouf, Carla. *Changing Veils: Women and Modernization in North Yemen*. Austin: University of Texas Press, 1979.

Malti-Douglas, Fedwa. *Woman's Word: Gender and Discourse in Arabo-Islamic Writing*. Princeton: Princeton University Press, 1991.

Masri, Abdullah H. O. ed. *An Introduction to the Antiquities of Saudi Arabia*. Riyadh: Department of Antiquities and Museums, 1975.

Masri, Abdullah H. O. *The Ancient and Historic Legacies of Saudi Arabia*. Washington, D.C.: Three Continents Press, 1979.

McLoughlen, Leslie. *Ibn Saud: Founder of a Kingdom*. New York: St. Martin's Press, 1993.

Mernissi, Fatima, trans. by Mary Jo Lakeland. *The Veil and the Male Elite: A Feminist Interpretation of Women's Rights in Islam*. Reading: Addison-Wesley Publishing Company, Inc., 1987.

Mernissi, Fatima. *Beyond the Veil: Male-Female Dynamics in Modern Muslim Society*. Bloomington: Indiana University Press, 1987.

Minai, Na'ila. Women in Islam. Seaview Press, 1981.

Mordechai, Abir. *Saudi Arabia: Society, Government and the Gulf Crisis*. New York: Routledge, 1993.

Naddaff, Sandra. *Arabesque: Narrative Structure and the Aesthetics of Repetition in 1001 Nights*. Evanston: Northwestern University Press, 1991.

Nydell, Margaret K. *Understanding Arabs*. Yarmouth: Intercultural Press, 1987.

Penault, David. *Story-telling Techniques in the Thousand and One Nights*. Leiden: E.J. Brill Publishers, 1991.

Presley, John R. and Rodney Wilson. *Search for Security: Saudi Arabian Oil and American Foreign Policy, 1939-1949*. Chapel Hill: University of North Carolina Press, 1991.

Pryce-Jones, David. *The Closed Circle: An Interpretation of the Arabs*. Wilmington: Harper and Rowe, 1989.

Rashid, Nasser I and Ibrahim Shaheen. *King Fahd and Saudi Arabia's Great Evolution*. Joplin: International Institute of Technology, 1987.

Reeves, Minou. *Female Warriors of Allah: Women and the Islamic Revolution*. New York: E. P. Dutton, 1989.

Sedat, Jihan. *A Woman in Egypt*. New York: Simon Schuster, 1987.

Shaarawi, Huda, trans. by Margot Badran. *Harem Years: The Memoirs of an Egyptian Feminist*. North Promfret: Virago Press, 1986.

Sowayan, Saad. *Nabati Poetry: The Oral Poetry of Arabia*. Berkeley: University of California Press, 1985.

Sowayan, Saad. *The Arabian Oral Historical Narrative: An Ethnographic and Linguistic Analysis*. Wiesbaden: Otta Harrassowtiz, 1992.

Stetkevych, Suzanne Pinckney. *Abu Tammam and the Poetics of the Abbasid Age*. Leiden: E.J. Brill Publishers, 1991.

Stetkevych, Suzanne Pinckney. *Reorientations: Studies in Arabic and Persian Poetry*. Bloomington: Indiana University Press, 1993.

Theroux, Peter. *Sandstorms: Days and Nights in Arabia.* New York: W. W. Norton and Company. 1990.

Viola, Joy W. *Human Resource Development in Saudi Arabia: Multinationals and Saudization.* Boston: International Human Resource Development Corporation, 1986.

Wikan, Unni. *Behind the Veil in Oman.* Baltimore: John Hopkins University Press, 1982.

Wilson, Rodney. *Banking and Finance in the Arab Middle East.* New York: St. Martin's Press, 1982.

Recent Dissertations by Saudi Writers

Alogla, Sulaiman Ibn Saleh, "Scientific and Technical Information Transfer: Promoting Information Aquisition in the Saudi Arabian Industrial Sector." Ph. D. dissertation. Indiana University. March 1993.

Al-Aiban, K. M., Ph.D. "The Effect of Economic Abundance and Scarcity on the Saudi Arabia Public Budget." University of California. 1991.

Asseri, Abdulrahman, Ph.D. "Familism and the Urbanization of Rural Villagers in the South Western Region of Saudi Arabia." Michigan State University. 1991.

Bazai, Hamad S., Ph.D. "Econometric Modelling of Consumption Behavior in Saudi Arabia: An Error Correction Approach." Colorado State University. 1991.

Dosary, Adel Shaheen, Ph.D. "Toward the Reduction of Foreign Workers in Saudi Arabia." University of Michigan 1991.

Al-Elg, Ali Habib, "Portfolio Consumption, branching, Ownership, Structure and Earnings: Evidence from Saudi Commercial Banks." Ph. D. dissertation. University of Mississippi. May 1993.

Fodah, Olfat M. Ph.D. "Measuring the Need for Computer Training for Educators in Saudi Arabia: Toward a Computer Training Model." University of Oregon. 1990

Hamoud, Ahmed, Ph.D. "The Reform of the Reform: A Critical and Empirical Assessment of the 1977 Saudi Civil Service Reform." University of Pittsburgh. 1991.

Al-Harbi, Abdullah J., "Manufacturing Strategy Priorities, Manufacturing Structure, and Business Performance: An Empirical Study Investigating Companies Operating in Saudi Arabia." Ph. D. dissertation. Southern Illinois University. March 1993.

Hazmi, Mubarak Wasel, Ph.D. "The Development of Public Relations in Saudi Arabia, A Survey." Wayne State University. 1990.

Al-Ismail, Hammad M., "The Impact of Advanced Technologies and Job-skill Requirements on Employee Job Productivity in Saudi Arabia's Petrochemical Industry." Ph. D. dissertation. Southern Illinios University. March 1993.

Jeaid, Khalid O., Ph.D. "Managerial Behavior in Saudi Arabia. Utilizing the Tempral Factor in the Analysis of Managerial Behavior." Florida State University. 1991.

Joma, Hesam Abdul Salam, Ph.D. "The Earth as Mosque: Integration of the Traditional Islamic Environmental Planning Ethnic with Agricultural and Water Development Policies in Saudi Arabia." University of Pennsylvania. 1991.

Moneef, N. M.. Ph.D. "The Development Process and its Relation to Oil Revenue and Dependence on Imported Labor in Saudi Arabia." University of Texas at Austin. 1991

Nafaieh, Dhaifallah A., Ph.D. "Privatization for Development: An Analysis of Potential Private Sector Participation in Saudi Arabia." University of Pittsburgh. 1990.

Sonbul, Saleh Ali, "Computer-based Technology Transfer: An Analysis of the Human Resource Dimension as it Relates to the Saudiization of CMIS Personnel in Saudi Arabia." Ph. D. dissertation., George Washington University. Feb. 1993.

Qahtani, Salem Saeed, Ph.D. "The Career Choice of Saudi Arabian Male Public Sector Employees." University of Pittsburgh. 1991.

About the Contributors and Editors

Abdulaziz Ibrahim Saleh Al-Sweel

Dr. Al-Sweel is currently the Director of Academic Affairs at the Saudi Arabian Cultural Mission to the United States in Washington, D.C. His office is responsible for the supervision of thousands of Saudi students who are pursuing academic degrees in the United States. He is also personally committed to the development of academic publications and educational programs on the Kingdom of Saudi Arabia for American audiences. His own vitae includes fourteen published articles and a host of reviews in a variety of journals and magazines. Before moving to Washington, D.C., Dr. Al-Sweel was Associate Professor in the Department of English at King Saud University in Riyadh, where he taught from 1983-1988. He received a Ph. D in linguistics from the University of Washington at Seattle in 1983.

Richard Bianchi

The Public Relations Coordinator for the Saudi Arabian Cultural Mission to the United States in Washington, D.C., Richard Bianchi acts as a liaison between the Mission and U.S. educational institutions, national and international organizations, and corporations. Several essays and editorials that he has edited or written have been published in newspapers and magazines. He is a graduate of the Columbia College School of Arts and Sciences at George Washington University, where his concentration was in Middle Eastern Affairs.

Andrew M. Evans

Andrew M. Evans is a research assistant in the Department of Business Management at Washington College, Chestertown, Maryland, where he specializes in topics related to the Arab region's economic development and commercial history. Recent projects have involved research and presentations on the United States Army Corps of Engineers' role in Saudi Arabian political-econmics during the 1980s, and analysis of the Kingdom's five-year development plans. He is currently active in a Council for the National Interests study on the feasibility for establishing direct lending facilities for Arab entrepreneurs in the occupied territories.

Jaafar Sheikh Idris

Jaafer Sheik Idris studied at the University of London from 1962-1964, and he later received a doctorate of philosophy degree from the University of

Khartoum in 1970. Following his graduation he taught at the Khartoum and in Umdurman in the Sudan from 1970-1973, and from 1972 to 1988 he taught at Imam Mohammed bin Saud Islamic University and King Saud University in Saudi Arabia. He is currently Director of the Research Center at the Institute of Islamic and Arabic Sciences in America. Dr. Idris has traveled widely in his position as an Islamic scholar, giving lectures at Islamic centers and universities in Africa, Australia, the Caribbean, the Middle East, and East Asia.

Adel A. Al-Jubeir

Adel A. Al-Jubeir is an assistant to His Royal Highness Prince Bandar bin Sultan. He received a Bachelor of Arts degree from North Texas University in 1982, graduating *summa cum laude*, and in 1984 he received a Master degree in international relations from Georgetown University. In 1986 Mr. Al-Jubeir was appointed to the senior staff of the Royal Embassy of Saudi Arabia to the United States as the Embassy's Congressional Liaison. During the Gulf crisis he was reassigned to Saudi Arabia to deal with the international news media. The following October he served as a member of the Gulf Cooperation Council's delegation to the Madrid Peace Talks. More recently, he was part of Saudi Arabia's delegation at the Multilateral Arms Control Talks.

Abdullah Hassan Othman Masry

Abdullah Hassan Othman Masry has received many honors and distinctions for his contributions to archeology, anthropology, and civil service. After his graduation from the University of California at Berkeley in 1967, he entered the University of Chicago's graduate program in anthropology. In 1971 he received his Master of Arts degree, and, following a research tour to Iraq, Iran, and Turkey, he completed his Ph. D. with a dissertation on "Prehistory in Northeast Saudi Arabia." In 1979, he published a book entitled *The Ancient and Historical Legacies of Saudi Arabia*. Dr. Masry has represented Saudi Arabia at UNESCO conferences to promote museum foundations, and he has participated as a government official at talks in Canada, Egypt, Germany, Jordan, Pakistan, Senegal, Sweden, Syria, Tunis, the United Kingdom, the United States, and Yemen.

Shiela Scoville

Dr. Scoville is currently an Academic Advisor at the Saudi Arabian Cultural Mission to the United States in Washington, D.C., where she also assists the Embassy with the development of outreach and publications materials. She has taught courses on the Middle East's culture and business environment and courses on Middle Eastern history at the American Graduate

School at Thunderbird, Arizona State University, the University of Arizona, and Phoenix College. She is the editor of Volume I of the five volume *Gazetteer of Arabia: A Geographical and Tribal History of the Arabian Peninsula*. She received her Ph.D. from UCLA in history in 1982.

Saad Abdullah Sowayan

Dr. Sowayan is an Associate Professor of Anthropology and Folklore at King Saud University in Riyadh. He received his Ph. D. in Interdisciplinary Studies from the University of California at Berkeley in 1982. Since then his articles on the subject of folk culture and popular literature in Saudi Arabia have been printed and quoted extensively in journals, newspapers, and magazines. He is a regular guest on television shows that are produced on Arab folk traditions, and he has been an active participant in the al-Jenadriyah festival. His major publications include *Nabati Poetry: The Oral Poetry of Arabia*, published by the University of California Press in 1985, and *The Arabian Oral Historical Narrative: An Ethnographic and Linguistic Analysis*, published in Wiesbaden by Otto Harrassowitz in 1992.

Anne Marie Weiss-Armush

Anne Marie Weiss-Armush is a journalist who lived with her husband in Jeddah and Al Khobar, Saudi Arabia, for eleven years. She continues to travel extensively in the Arab region, particularly to Syria, were her husband's family lives in a village outside Damascus. Ms. Weiss-Armush has served as a correspondent for *The Arab News* and *The Saudi Gazette*, and she has been the focus of two culinary-oriented television documentaries made for Saudi Channel Two. Her first book, *Arabian Cuisine*, which was published in 1984, will be followed by a book presently in press at Lowell House. She writes for the *Dallas Morning News* and is a consultant for Aramco and the International Business Center in Dallas, Texas.

J. W. Wright, Jr.

J. W. Wright is a Professor of Business Management at Washington College in Chestertown, Maryland, where he specializes in research on Arab and Islamic economies. He has given lectures on Arab-related topics at Cambridge University, Indiana University, and the University of Chicago, the University of Jordan, St. Andrews University, the World Bank, and he has taught in training programs for the Saudi Arabian Agricultural Bank. Professor Wright has published several articles on Arab cultures and economies. In March of 1993 he was made a Malone Fellow for Arab and Islamic Studies by the National Council for U.S.-Arab Relations.

NAME & SUBJECT INDEX